Professional Practice

Professional Practice

A Guide to Turning Designs Into Buildings

W · W · Norton & Company

New York · London

Paul Segal, FAIA

For information about permission to reproduce selections from this book,
write to Permissions, W. W. Norton & Company, Inc., 500 Fifth Avenue,
New York, NY 10110.

Manufacturing by LSC Crawfordsville
Composition by Ken Gross
Book design by Antonina Krass
Production manager: Leeann Graham

Library of Congress Cataloging-in-Publication Data

Segal, Paul.
   Professional practice : a guide to turning designs into buildings / Paul
Segal.
       p.   cm.
   Includes index.
   ISBN-13: 978-0-393-73180-4 (pbk.)
   ISBN-10: 0-393-73180-4 (pbk.)
   1. Architectural practice—United States. 2. Architectural services market-
ing—United States. I. Title.
NA1996.S44 2006
720.68'8—dc22   200505849

ISBN 13: 978-0-393-73180-4 (pbk.)
ISBN 10: 0-393-73180-4 (pbk.)

W. W. Norton & Company, Inc., 500 Fifth Avenue, New York, N.Y. 10110
www.wwnorton.com

W. W. Norton & Company Ltd., 15 Carlisle Street, London
W1T 3BS

0 9 8 7 6 5

Contents

Preface

After teaching the Professional Practice course at Columbia University Graduate School of Architecture, Planning and Preservation (GSAPP) for almost twenty years, I realized that one of the biggest problems with the course has been the lack of a textbook that covers the topic succinctly and from an average practitioner's point of view—warts and all, the exhilarating parts and the disappointing parts. One of the advantages of teaching this course, subtitled Turning Designs into Buildings, is that it benefits from a very low level of expectation from the students. Typical end-of-year course evaluations begin with "I expected this course to be painfully boring, but since it was required for graduation I had to take it, and it actually was a lot better than I expected." While having no desire to become an author, I really wanted there to be a good book for this course, a variation of which every architecture student has to take. Maybe a shorter (not to mention lighter) book than the alternative would be appreciated.

When James Polshek was dean at Columbia GSAPP and hired me, he broke with the tradition of selecting the business partner of a large firm to teach Professional Practice and instead chose a practicing architect (me) more interested in and known for *design* than for *business*. Jim wisely suggested that the focus be what architects should know to protect their designs, from concept through comple-

tion. These issues have been central to my courses, and they are basic to this book.

The second purpose of the course and of this book is to persuade architects, starting during their education and carrying through their time as employees and even as principals, should they elect to practice on their own or in a group, that they add value to the building endeavor—for the client and for society. This sounds lofty. It is. It is also, when architecture is done right, true. Good planning and careful, thoughtful design help clients utilize all their resources—the land, materials, time, money, and effort that go into a project—more efficiently and wisely and obtain a result that is more suitable and efficient for its purpose, more durable and maintainable, and a timeless source of joy for the users.

Understanding planning and design issues, and how the services to accomplish them are provided, is essential. Explaining these issues clearly to clients is critical. If clients' expectations match our efforts, they will not be disappointed; they will appreciate our work on their behalf. To the extent that there is a difference between what they think we will do for them and what we want to and can do for them, that difference between expectation and reality will always be a problem. If clients think we can guarantee a contractor's work, they will be angry at us when they find we can't. (I will explain how to get the best possible results from a contractor in a variety of situations, but that is very different from a *guarantee*.)

A few comments about the contents of this book. While I often say, "Here is the way something should be done" (or not done), does that mean it is actually the only way it should be done, or that it should always be done that way? Absolutely not! One of the basic aspects of being a professional is that every circumstance should be carefully examined and considered, to see if the general response or action (which is what I will discuss in the following chapters) is appropriate, or whether the specific situation requires a different answer. Being a thoughtful professional includes evaluating many situations that are not at all black-and-white. (If they were, we could be replaced by well-programmed robots.) Lots of issues are gray, with many shades and nuances. This makes practice complicated. Which is what makes it interesting!

You will notice there is no chapter (or even section) entitled Ethics. Do not construe this omission as a lack of interest in the subject on my part. Rather, it is based on a firm belief that ethical behavior is a core part of a professional's entire life and imbues all activities and actions. I allude to ethics in many places: treatment of clients, staff, and society; disclosure of possible conflicts of interest; design considerations of the planet's resources; fees for services; competitions; and behavior by and to professionals. Ethics always boils down to a few fundamentals—treating others as you would like them to treat you, being honest and forthright, and serving your clients' and society's interests. Being ethical will definitely provide you with more success and fun as an architect. (If you don't feel comfortable about doing something, or wouldn't want anyone to know what you are doing, then please consider whether you should be doing it at all.)

A long and complex process takes place between the time you sketch and model an idea and the time you can walk around in its finished manifestation. I have tried to explain the various steps in a short and simple text. I hope you have as much fun reading it as I did writing it, and as I do teaching it. And I hope that learning how to practice professionally helps you love doing architecture as much as I do.

Acknowledgments

Many people contributed to the stew of ideas that make up this book, from my early childhood to last week. I thank:

Our clients, whose trust and optimism give us the reasons to practice, and from whom we have learned so much about so many fields.

Our talented and dedicated office colleagues over the last thirty-five years, with whom we have shared the excitement and lessons of practice, many still working with us, many now heads of their own successful offices (probably our best accomplishment).

Our many consultants who have shared their expertise and judgment with us, among them especially structural engineer Robert Silman, who has helped us for over thirty years, and construction attorney Larry Gainen, who has provided business and legal wisdom; I am grateful that all have as much common sense and thoughtfulness as technical knowledge.

The associated architects with whom we have shared work on projects, and from whom we had great lessons in professionalism, particularly Elliott Glass, Barton Myers, and Bernie Rothzeid and his partners.

The contractors we have worked with, whose management skills, construction knowledge, drive, and enthusiasm have helped us serve our clients and realize our projects, and the skilled craftspeople who have added their personal skills, commitment, and expertise, all necessary to create high quality construction.

My friends and colleagues at the AIA New York Chapter, with whom I have worked for the betterment of the profession: Peter Samton, a true mentor; Randy Croxton and Bart Voorsanger, who have shared the leadership trenches with me; David Spector, who led me to writing this book.

Columbia University Graduate School of Architecture, Planning and Preservation, where I have been privileged to teach practice for twenty years; James Polshek, the dean who hired me; Bernard Tschumi and Mark Wigley, the deans who kept me; and all the bright and inquiring students of that great school.

My teachers at Princeton University School of Architecture, notably Michael Graves and Charles Gwathmey, who inspired their students to be teaching-architects and architects for whom architecture is life, not just a profession.

The people who helped this book happen: my former student and office colleague, Emily Sobel; my thorough researcher and text assistant, Zsuzsanna Vig; and particularly my editor at W. W. Norton, Nancy Green, whose elegant editing, clear questioning, and always excellent taste made writing this book one of the most interesting and rewarding experiences of my life.

My family: my sister Susan, a woman of intellect and skill in putting social concerns into action; my children, Emma and Sarah, who inform me of another generation's perspective and concerns and keep me (and everyone else) from taking things too seriously, and for whom I want the readers of this book to make a better world; my mother, who taught me the importance of values and kindness; my father, who taught me almost everything I know other than architecture, whose wisdom I draw on liberally in this book and who is the best role model any son could have; my wife, Christine, a woman of intellectual brilliance, personal compassion, and uncanny clarity and ability to get-it-done.

Finally, Michael Pribyl, my partner in practice for thirty-five years and college and architecture school classmate before that—the reason I always say "we" instead of "I" when talking about practice. He is a man of great design talent and integrity, whom I feel privileged and honored to call my partner.

1 About the Profession

People build buildings because they have a need that has to be met. A company is growing and needs a new factory or offices. A religious congregation is growing (or shrinking) and needs a new place of worship. A family buys a country property and needs a vacation house. Probably no one builds merely for the fun of it. (Although, other than having and bringing up children, to me nothing is more fun and satisfying than building things!) It is expensive and time consuming, and it takes tremendous effort. Still, a lot gets built—some wonderful, but most mundane. Often the former is called "architecture" and the latter "construction."

What do architects do? The general public, by and large, doesn't know. Clients who are otherwise quite sophisticated people have asked me, "Do you make blueprints?" Well, the firm creates designs, which become drawings from which blueprint copies are made. But that's not really accurate: blueprinting, a copying method, has not even been available for almost forty years. To start with, architecture is a profession. What does that mean?

What Is a Profession?

In his address at the opening of the forerunner of the School of Social Work at Columbia University in 1915, noted educator

Abraham Flexner listed six attributes that he felt defined a profession as opposed to other kinds of vocation. A *profession*

1. involves a store of knowledge that is more than ordinarily complex;

2. is an intellectual enterprise;

3. applies theoretical and complex knowledge to the solution of human and social problems;

4. strives to add to and improve the stock of knowledge;

5. passes its knowledge to novice generations, usually through universities; and

6. tends to organize in peer formations that establish criteria for admission, practice, and conduct.

A professional must be imbued with an altruistic spirit, the desire to serve as well as to reap profit. "Professional" is the antonym of "commercial."

In an age when practitioners of many vocations want to define themselves as professionals, I always go back to Flexner's six points.

How is architecture doing as a profession in Flexner's terms? In some ways it is doing very well (1, 2, and 3) in my view; some areas have room for improvement (4 and 5); and in one area (6) the profession has partly ceded responsibility to the government—licensing.

Licensing

The purpose of licensing is to fulfill the government's job of protecting public health, safety, and welfare. As with many issues in which the government becomes involved, some people think this is an intrusion into personal rights. Where does the government get off telling me what I can do with my work (licensing)? With my property/land (zoning)?

The average person has no way of knowing whether or not someone offering services to the public, whether architectural, legal, or medical, is reasonably (or even minimally) qualified to do so. It is reasonable for the government to help by, in effect, certifying that certain people have the training, experience, and character to hold themselves qualified to provide those services.

Typically, with regard to professions, state governments regulate two issues: what people are permitted to *call* themselves and what people are permitted to *do*. These are the two usual parts of professional licensing laws, called "title acts" (what you are allowed to call yourself) and "practice acts" (what you are allowed to do). The states, not the American Institute of Architects (AIA) or the federal government, grant licenses. Various states have organized to help test and accredit individuals via the National Council of Architectural Registration Boards (NCARB), but each individual state still issues the licenses that permit architects to call themselves architects and to do those things considered to constitute the practice of architecture.

In most states one earns a license by

1. meeting educational requirements by obtaining a professional degree from an accredited program in an academic institution (some states permit, in lieu of a degree, a "learning equivalency" earned by a long period of work for a licensed architect);

2. obtaining practical experience by working for a licensed architect, usually for three years, sometimes called an internship;

3. passing a series of licensing examinations, often the Architectural Registration Examinations (AREs), written under the auspices of NCARB and administered and graded by each state; and

4. assuring good character (that is, demonstrating that you have character, not are a character).

In a growing number of states the NCARB's Intern Development Program (IDP) is used to help track each aspiring architect's practical learning phase, to be sure that the candidate has been exposed to and participated in the many facets of the profession during internship and has not spent three years drawing stair details and nothing else.

To maintain a license, typically a licensed architect must maintain a good standard of practice, conform to the particular state's rules of conduct, and, in some states, participate in continuing education, to sustain the goal of life-long learning. And pay the state's licensing fee.

Since licensing is a state function, you must contact your state's licensing body to find out its specific requirements for earning and maintaining licensure.

The Profession's Place in the American Psyche

Probably no book (or movie, depending on your media preference) has had as much influence on what people think about the profession of architecture as Ayn Rand's *The Fountainhead*, written over half a century ago. The hero, Howard Roark, is a talented, uncompromising loner. A powerfully painted character, he is no doubt the model for many architects, indeed a whole culture of individuals in the profession. The book has also played a part in what the public knows about—and thinks of—architects. Roark is compelling and romantic, a man who forges ahead with an idea he sees as vital, true, and right, but that the client (or general public) doesn't quite get yet. Sometimes this is a useful approach, but it is also one that can be irrelevant and counterproductive to successfully achieving your own architectural ideas in the twenty-first century. Today architects play a pivotal role in the largest segment of the American economy,

construction. In this position architects are called upon to master huge amounts of complex (and often contradictory) information, create solutions that are multidimensional and multifaceted, and orchestrate a wide variety of players to convert those ideas into a built work. This is not a job that can be done by a pig-headed individualist. It is a job that calls for people who can communicate their ideas clearly and convincingly, who can forge mutually beneficial alliances among disparate parties, and who can understand and enforce complex legal and contractual relationships to get things done. Architects today need to possess a virtually renaissance range of skills or participate in teams that work in complementary, respectful, coordinated ways.

The Roark personality is often promoted in architecture school culture as the "true way." This is damaging to students for many reasons. It teaches that the only desirable goal is to become that individualistic practitioner who knows better than everyone else and will succeed by forcing his or her beliefs on an ignorant public. This is not a formula for a successful, happy, or constructive life, or for actually getting anything done.

Richard Swett, a former ambassador to Denmark and former congressman from New Hampshire, the only architect to serve in the U.S. Congress in the twentieth century, believes that architectural training and experience are the best preparation you can have for solving a wide range of society's problems—not just for building things. I agree: good architects learn

1. to educate themselves quickly to solve new problems (every time you get a project that is a new building type or context, you must quickly learn a lot) and to analyze a great deal of data, often incomplete or conflicting;

2. to create ideas that synthesize the information, often using other seemingly unrelated arts or technologies;

3. to communicate those ideas verbally and graphically into an action, or "how to do it," plan;

4. to figure out the best process for implementing the ideas; and

5. to get it done, as conceived, often utilizing entities who have conflicting interests.

These are the tools needed to solve every type of complex problem—business, social, or governmental. While architects get great training to do many things, school culture on the Roark model tries to force us all into one narrow little box. Graduating architecture students should look hard at their own personalities and interests and seek to use their skills in the best-suited ways. Consider working for entities other than architects' offices: think of developers, contractors, government, corporations, or educational institutions. Take off the blinders! You can do a lot of satisfying and useful things with an architec-

tural education besides trying to be Howard Roark. (He didn't end up all that happy.)

Architecture as a Design Service Business

For an architectural practice to be *successful* (a word that has a very broad meaning, as will become apparent), it must combine design, service, and business, the supports of a three-legged stool. Without all three working well, the enterprise falls down.

By *design* I mean the full range of planning for the best utilization of all a client's (and society's) resources, including land, labor, time, energy, and money. It is in consideration of design in this fullest sense, not just as appearance (also important, but not exclusively), that design becomes rich and useful. Design calls for juggling six balls in the air, not just one. Consideration of multiple issues makes the endeavor more complicated but ultimately produces a better end product (probably richer visually as well) and thus is more rewarding.

Service has three components. First is *independence*, also known as integrity. The sole purpose of the advice an architect gives to a client should be that it is in the best interests of the client and of society: the architect shouldn't have a separate agenda (like fame and publicity, unless that is explicitly what the client wants) or receive any financial benefit for services other than what the client directly pays the architect in fees. While most state licensing laws forbid such extra payments, the issue should be more basic to an architect's method of operation. Charging finder's fees, sharing contractors' profits for a job that runs smoothly, accepting rebates from suppliers or manufacturers are all unacceptable. A simple test for an offered benefit is to ask yourself whether you would feel comfortable having your client know about it, and whether you would be happy to see it on the front page of the *New York Times* (or the paper of your choice) tomorrow. If the answer to either question is no, then you should reconsider the offer. When in doubt, discuss the issue fully and openly with your client. Disclosure solves many potential problems.

For example, once I was one of a small group of architects and designers acting as a consultant to the Formica Corporation, advising on products and marketing. Whenever our firm specified a Formica product on a project, I discussed my consultancy role with the client. For my work at Formica I was paid a consultant's fee, so whether more or less of the product was sold was of no economic interest to me (not to mention the total insignificance to Formica of the quantities I was specifying). Still, full disclosure to clients of the possible appearance of a conflict of interest is the best policy.

Architects have an excellent record of avoiding conflict of interest, maintaining high standards of business conduct, and acting honorably. This is what makes our advice valuable to clients. This is not always true in other professions. An example is doctors who prescribe medications from companies for which they do paid research, without disclosing this connection to their patients. Another example is some accountants who have charged their clients huge fees for tax avoidance strategies they know were questionable.

The second component of service is *usefulness*. It should be obvious, but is sometimes overlooked, that architects are hired to solve clients' problems in the best, most efficient way. Such solutions should be original, inventive, even uplifting. Being useful to a client is not mundane. It is necessary.

The third component of service is *reliability*: getting things done on time and on budget. I've never heard a client say, "Well, the architect got it done on time and on budget, but I didn't like the design." Too often architects who have delivered wonderful, creative solutions end up with clients who would never hire them again (or didn't even build that project) because the architect's work was late or the budgets weren't met and there were substantial cost overruns. These are bad, and avoidable, reasons to fail. Schedules and budgets are real and important to clients; failing to meet them has quantifiable, negative impact. If you think clients will forgive you for late, over-budget projects because the finished design is brilliant, think again.

To succeed professionally you must deliver design, provide service, and maintain a functioning **business**. Over a given period you need to make a profit–that is, have more income than expenses. You must develop enough capital to invest in staff development and training, equipment (more hardware and software), and the workplace (the office), and have a cushion to ride through the slow times, which are inevitable in a profession that is closely tied to a cyclical economy. You need the resources to explore and hone design solutions and the time and expertise to execute them well. Good design and service will definitely help make a business succeed and last.

Ultimately architects running a practice must have several goals, some of which may at times seem to be conflicting, but which are mutually supporting in the long term:

- serving clients
- training young architects
- providing a challenging and satisfying work environment
- making a fair profit

Pluses and Minuses of the Profession

Every profession has advantages and disadvantages. Some of the pluses of being an architect include the following:

- creating works that people use and enjoy and that enhance their lives and environment

- creating works that last beyond the act of service: you can revisit buildings many years after your efforts and see the fruits of those efforts being used
- contributing to one of the most lasting records of human society and being part of a long chain of people leaving those marks
- being a member of a profession that enjoys a reputation for integrity (a recent Lou Harris poll showed "architect" as the second most respected of about forty vocations)
- enjoying importance while preserving your anonymity

In a world where so many people want to be recognized, the last item may sound weird. I once had a very famous client. When I walked down the street with him, passersby stopped and cars screeched to a halt. He might have loved it, even needed the attention. If that were my life, I'd hate it. I've also walked down the street with I. M. Pei and with Gordon Bunshaft, two famous architects of the second half of the twentieth century, and nobody noticed.

Looking at the minuses of the profession is a more interesting roadmap of what needs to be done to improve it, discussed in the conclusion to this book.

The value of what architects add to a project is not well understood, and therefore not appreciated or rewarded. After teachers, architects probably have the lowest ratio of "value added" to "compensation." (What does this say about people who teach architecture?)

Architects are selling something that is invisible to most of our society, which, sadly, is fairly visually illiterate. Most people learn computational and reading and writing skills all the way through high school but stop learning how to look in second grade. Trying to sell good design is like trying to sell books or magazines to a world in which no one can read. It is a tough sale.

Other than with relatively small projects such as private custom houses, there is usually a separation between architects and most end users of buildings—the real consumers of our services. Our actual clients are almost always intermediaries—a developer, a corporation, a government. You know who your doctor is—he talks to you, examines you, advises you. It's different with architects. Most of the people who use the buildings we design haven't a clue about who the architects were, what they did, or how the buildings got to be the way they are.

Goals

When I first started teaching, a student asked me what my goals in practice were. It's something I had never really thought much about, but all architects should consider the question seriously. My priorities then (and now) are as follows:

- to create high-quality, thoughtful, and appropriate work
- to provide a beneficial service to clients and the public
- to make an enjoyable workplace, working for people and with people I like and respect, in a place that pleases me and in which I want to spend my time
- to earn a decent living

What do *you* want to do? Where do you want to be in five, ten, or twenty years? Your aims may be very different from mine. Knowing your own goals will help you achieve them.

Questions for You

People often follow an unconscious career path of least resistance. It is a momentous decision to go to architecture school, and architecture students by all accounts work harder, with more all-nighters, than almost anyone else. How you make the decisions that shape your career is sometimes not as well thought through. You can take lots of different useful directions with an architect's training. The first step to finding the place that is best for you is to know yourself and understand the implications of your decisions.

What do you like to do and what are you best at? Some people are more intuitive, some more analytic; some are more artistic, some more technically minded; some work better in groups, some alone;

some like managing things, some don't. For each of those alternatives (and many more) there is a place or a role that will be well or poorly suited for you. If you prefer a stable environment, consider working for a large firm with the likelihood of consistent employment. If you like adventure and variety, a smaller firm is more likely to provide that. If you are a generalist who enjoys learning new things all the time, go to a firm that does a wide variety of building types and scales; if you like honing your skills and becoming expert in one thing, a firm that specializes in one building type will be a better fit. Geography—big city or small—sometimes plays a part in the scale and diversity of a firm's projects. Do you crave the buzz of city life or the quiet of country living? How do you feel about commuting?

Consider each of these (and other) issues, and be honest about which feels like the best fit for you (not for Howard Roark—you're probably pretty different from him). Make your decisions in an informed way, not by the fashion of school culture or by default.

2 The Parties in the Construction Industry

A very complex activity, building necessarily involves a lot of different people. They are divided into several basic groups, which have different functions. Their relationships are fairly standardized and usually contractual, and a full understanding of them is essential to professional practice. The groups are often known as "parties" in the construction industry; alas, I'm not talking about the caviar-and-champagne, or even chips-and-crudités, opening parties.

The three primary parties are the *owners* (often known to architects as the clients), the *design professionals* (including, of course, the architects), and the *constructors* (some of whom are contractors). In addition, a lot of other people, not in these three groups, are responsible for obtaining and providing the money with which to build projects; for writing and administering the laws and regulations that govern land use, design, construction, and building use; and for marketing real estate. Let's discuss the three primary parties first.

Owners/Clients

There are many different kinds of clients, with very different goals and methods of operating. The kind of client you work with can make a project a wonderful experience or a total misery. To a degree the outcome, and the level of fit or misfit between the client and the architect, can be predicted by understanding the motives and interests of the range of clients and by being honest and realistic about yourself and your firm. Some owner/architect combinations are made in heaven; some . . . well, you know what I mean.

Private Clients

Private clients who build for themselves are known as *owner-users*. Private owners who build for other people are called *developers*.

Private owner-users can be individuals, who might be commissioning a house for themselves; corporations, which may want a new office building, factory, or retail store; or institutional clients, such as private schools, universities, hospitals, or religious entities, commissioning buildings for themselves. Designing a home for its users has the potential advantage of a very close designer-user connection, allowing, without translation by intermediaries, communication of the goals and constraints, the program, and the finances. A one-on-one relationship, it can last beyond the job. It is rewarding to see people whom you like and care about enjoying the results of your work; it provides important feedback about spaces and relationships of spaces to each other and to the landscape, about what works and what doesn't, and about how your intentions became (or didn't become) reality.

Such a close relationship also can have pitfalls. Our firm once designed very complicated offices for a company moving to New

York. After a smooth, fast, and on-budget construction phase, the company moved in to great success, delight, and favorable publicity. Soon after, we were asked to design a high-end apartment renovation for the company owner, while the couple lived in the apartment. The project was as great a disaster as the office was a success. Everything went wrong—endless client change orders, damage to property that was not moved out of the way of construction, and more. A strong architect/client relationship built on one kind of project was destroyed by the different nature of another—same people, different kind of project. (The experience taught me to tell clients that construction is like surgery—painful but beneficial—and that living in a construction site is like surgery without anesthesia. Not advisable.)

Corporate owner-users range from companies building large projects for the first time, with a lot at stake and very little in-house expertise to manage it (or that outsource facilities management to owner's representatives, discussed below), to corporations (typically larger and more established) that build frequently and have in-house facilities-management staffs, often very experienced, and often including licensed architects. Corporate clients are really in some other business, which is their main focus and interest.

With first-time corporate clients, it is essential for the architect to understand senior management's objectives and knowledge of the design and construction process. If their knowledge is limited, the architect must fully educate the client so expectations and reality coincide. Small corporations may be run by the people who are the major owners. In large corporations, the management is usually hired by a board of directors that is elected by the shareholders. The coincidence or distance of ownership to management can have a big impact on the professional services involved with these major corporate commitments of financial resources.

In the 1980s our firm designed offices for a lot of midsized advertising agencies that needed new offices because they were expanding fast. All the agencies were owned by the people who ran them. While individually very different, these people shared certain characteristics: they were all very smart, learned rapidly about new topics (such as architecture), could focus sharply on alternatives and the pros and cons of each, understood the nexus of art and business, and appreciated the influence that design could have in serving their purposes. Those projects were a perfect marriage of architect and client—fun, creative, constructive, fast, and profitable. The clients were open to new ideas and experimentation, and we all benefited. I learned that a project that works out well for one party works well for the other. It's always a two-way street.

Our firm likes working for private owner-user clients because they often plan to own their projects for a long time, and thus they are interested in durability, energy conservation, and avoiding faddish designs—goals compatible with ours. They can make decisions quickly and understand the consequences of making changes (almost always harmful on projects). They also understand the value of investing in quality, because they are the beneficiaries.

Institutional clients are usually not-for-profit entities, such as private educational, research, foundation, health, or religious groups. They are motivated by purposes other than profit (which is not to say they don't care about the economics of a project). They usually intend to own their projects for a long time and care about multiple interests of their constituencies. They often have caring and thoughtful leadership whose motives mirror the positive and constructive purposes of the institution.

Developers are a subcategory of private owners, individuals or companies who build with the intention of owning and renting the properties or of selling the properties, sometimes even before the completion of construction. The projects, whether to be leased or sold, may be residential (single or multifamily) or commercial, such as offices or retail space. In the United States commercial developments are commonly leased. Single-family residential developments are usually built to be sold, while multifamily dwellings are built both ways—garden and high-rise apartments are rented, some are sold as condominiums (and as "cooperatives" in a few markets).

What does this mean for the architect? Personally I prefer clients who intend to own rather than sell because their interests are more likely to match my professional interest. (In support of this view, as noted in chapter 10, insurance companies that offer professional liability coverage for architects charge more if an architecture firm provides services for developers that build condominiums, on the presumption that the developer may ask the architect to specify inferior materials and systems, and may not even follow the architect's plans. These actions reduce the developer's costs but are likely to result in buildings that have deficiencies that may be the basis of lawsuits, often against the architect.)

Public Clients

Public clients are the other segment of the client group. They include governmental bodies at the federal, state, and local level. They commission huge amounts of construction, including infrastructure, such as roads, water and sewage systems, and transportation systems. These projects are mainly designed by civil engineers of various disciplines. Governments also build offices, schools, post offices, sports facilities, housing, military buildings, and transit stations, which are designed mainly by architects and represent a large percentage of the construction in the American economy. The public segment serves large numbers of people and plays an important civic and community role.

Public clients possess a wide latitude of degree of commitment to high-quality design and construction. The Brooks Bill, named for Congressman Jack Brooks of Texas and passed by Congress in 1970, mandates that architects for federal buildings be selected on the basis of design quality and that a fair fee be negotiated after their selection. This is a very different process of selection from one in which professional service providers are chosen on the basis of which one offers the lowest bid (a process you would not likely use to select a doctor or lawyer). Some programs, such as the federal government's General Services Administration's (GSA) Design Excellence program, have over the last decade been responsible for hiring some of the best architects in the country. Design Excellence supports with money, expertise, and commitment the design and construction of very fine courthouses and other federal buildings.

As with private clients, an architect must know the nature of the goals, process, mandate, and commitment of any governmental body and staff. These issues have a meaningful impact on the project.

Remember: architects are not obligated to take any client who wants to hire them. Other than for prejudicial reasons, such as race, religion, ethnicity, or gender preference, you have the right to reject any potential commission. Smart architects are highly selective in accepting clients. A good rule of thumb was articulated by I. M. Pei, who wisely counseled, "Go after the client, not the project." Our firm has done better work, had more fun, and made more profit from small jobs with good clients than from huge jobs with bad clients. Check every potential new client. Contact other professionals they have worked with; find out if they have been involved in a lot of litigation, particularly in construction or with other professionals. Clients always check *your* references; you should always check *theirs*. Trust your instincts. Many architects say, at the end of a bad project, "I knew that things didn't smell right with this client, but I wanted the project so badly, I went into it anyway." What a mistake!

So what makes a good client? In my opinion, whether the job is large or small, the same criteria always apply: mutual respect, enthusiasm for and openness to new possibilities, knowing their real goals and being able to articulate them, being clear about their resources, and having expectations that match. Bad clients think they know everything and are secretive, distrustful, and untrustworthy (actually, that sounds like bad employers, bad employees, bad friends, bad spouses, bad anyone). Naïve clients, who lack knowledge of the process and business experience, and who often have unrealistic expectations, can be problematic. Such clients engender more disputes and lawsuits than experienced clients. Be wary of a potential client whose opening remarks are about how dumb all his previous architects were.

In evaluating clients, look for their positions on issues such as long-term versus short-term ownership (life-cycle costs vs. first costs). Whether it's the clients' money or someone else's money being spent, are they going to maintain the buildings themselves or pass along those costs? Are their goals civic or selfish? How do the answers fit with your goals?

Design Professionals

Design professionals are all the people who produce (by art, design, invention, experience, and research) the information from which buildings are created: the architects, the engineers, and all the additional consultants who typically provide specialized knowledge about building systems or construction processes.

Architects

First in this group are the architects. (I know you're saying, "Hey, he didn't put us first at all—he put the owners first." Well, sorry to say, without the owners there are usually no projects for the architects. So: first among the design professionals, okay?)

Architects serve two main functions. We are the creators, the designers, the authors, and the coordinators of all the other design professionals' work. In these roles we take the information about the project's needs (the program), we synthesize this information (along with that of the site) into designs, we elaborate on those designs, and we produce working drawings and specifications that fully communicate what the owner contracts with the contractor to build, and exactly how to build it. Our second role (discussed in chapter 5), subtly different from the first, is to provide construction administration—that is, to guide the construction to a successful completion, consistent with the design intent, and to administer the owner/contractor agreement even-handedly to both parties.

Sometimes architecture firms join with other architecture firms to provide services for a specific project, to combine different areas of expertise, or to provide local expertise. Firms may partner for one project, in an association known as a *joint venture*, or form other forms of relationships, such as that of *associated architects*.

Today construction of all but the simplest buildings is far too complex for any individual to be proficient in all its aspects. Architects must be familiar enough with all the systems and all the processes by which buildings get built and then operate efficiently to organize, guide, evaluate, and incorporate the work of many others. It is a critical role, and it takes a broad understanding and general knowledge of technical and operational issues. It also calls for leadership ability and skill in team-building, group motivation, and management of multiple entities over a period of time to achieve common objectives. No wonder Howard Roark isn't the ideal prototype for a modern architect.

Engineers

Many kinds of engineers are involved in designing and creating buildings. Most are trained in subspecialties of civil engineering (as opposed to chemical, hydraulic, and aeronautical engineers; although these and virtually every other kind of engineer do play a role in some aspects of buildings, they are not among the ones architects work with most). The two kinds of engineers we work with most often are structural engineers and MEPS (mechanical, electrical, plumbing, and sprinkler) engineers. Most architects have learned enough about these disciplines in school and in practice to be able to do the relatively simple work involved in houses or other small buildings. But our firm always uses both kinds of engineers even in small projects, if only to confirm our advice. Never hesitate to admit you don't know enough about something and need some outside advice to give your client the best information.

Structural engineers help select the best and most appropriate structural system for a specific building and its context. The economics of the location, current market conditions of different materials, labor supply and expertise, and proximity to different supply and fabrication resources are all topics that good engineers consider in their choices of systems and subsystems. They evaluate such issues as size of structural column bays, the desirability of regular column spacing or the acceptability (or even preference, as in apartment house construction) of irregular column spacing, and the trade-offs of structural depth for increased bay sizes versus cost of structure. They determine the required strength, size, and shape of each component as well as all the connections, the fabrication and erection processes, the requisite testing at various stages, and the analysis of the test results to ensure that the requirements have been met.

Although structural engineers often also design the foundation systems for buildings, they formulate those designs based on information provided by others: test pits by surveyors in simple situations; data provided by soils engineers from borings, test pits, and core samples in more complex cases. When site conditions warrant it, structural engineers utilize the services of *foundations engineers* who specialize in the design of complex foundations, on difficult subsurface conditions (such as unstable or infirm soils; over tunnels, sewer lines, or other utilities) or when very close to other structures. When these subconsultants are used, the structural engineer oversees, coordinates, and reviews their work, but the architect must know enough to understand the issues, watch over the process, and give the owner an informed opinion on alternatives being considered.

The various MEPS engineering jobs, as well as fire safety and sometimes data and communications infrastructure, are usually done by different engineers, within the same firm by tradition, for ease of communications and coordination.

Mechanical engineers design the heating, ventilating, and air-conditioning (HVAC) systems. They research and analyze the specific macro- and microclimatic conditions of the site and the degree to which the building's design reduces the need to mechanically overcome environmental conditions. Good engineers work closely and collaboratively with architects to advise how to design the building to reduce its needs for energy-consuming systems, helping the project achieve lower first costs by reducing the amount of equipment needed and operating and repair costs. This up-front thinking benefits the owner (as well as the planet). Mechanical engineers consider alternative energy sources (electricity, oil, gas, solar, geothermal, wind, or tidal) as well as direct uses of these sources; alternative conversion and distribution systems of cooling and heating media, as well as the control systems to keep building users comfortable both individually and collectively, with the most cost-effective system to install and operate. Once systems are selected, mechanical engineers design, size, and specify the equipment and the control and distribution systems. They help to get the systems up and running by overseeing adjustments and balancing, all parts of commissioning. They teach the building owner how to use and maintain the systems.

In addition, mechanical engineers consider size and space efficiency, acoustical properties, maintenance ease and cost, and pollution factors. Mechanical systems are about the most demanding in terms of first cost, operating cost, and space required (both for the central equipment and for the distribution systems). The importance of their work may be gauged by the fact that the HVAC system and its controls are the topics that building users usually complain about the most. Architects rarely hear that "this building is very comfortable, never too hot, too cold, or too drafty, but I really don't like the structural system." (If you do hear that, go directly to the section in chapter 10 about professional liability insurance!)

Electrical engineers analyze a building's electrical needs and the available outside utility resources and design the connections to outside utilities, the electrical rooms where the power is divided and sent to the distribution systems, the emergency backup systems (if any) of batteries or generators, and the power control and protection subsystems.

Electrical engineers often handle the electrical portions of a building's life-safety systems, such as fire- and smoke-alarm systems. These include the devices that sense problems (temperature and smoke detectors in rooms or return air ducts, or that are connected to other systems, such as the sprinkler system in which they set off alarms when they detect a flow, indicating a head has gone off), the central control panels in a building, connections to outside monitoring companies or agencies, and devices such as horns, strobes, and speakers that communicate with building occupants.

Electrical engineers sometimes perform lighting-design services. They may be well qualified and skilled at the artistic as well as the technical aspects of lighting design, including knowledge of fixtures' design and performance characteristics.

Data and communications systems (data com) is another subspecialty that electrical engineers sometimes handle. The meaning of data engineering is rapidly changing; it currently includes selection, connection, equipment specification, and distribution networks of low-voltage systems such as T1 fiberoptics or Category 6 cabling, and microwave and wireless, which carry data. Data com is also known as IT (information technology) or MIS (management information systems). The names changes as fast as the field does. Communications, which to some extent is converging with data, includes the connections to outside sources and utilities, the equipment, and the distribution, both wired and wireless. When data com is very complex, or when the electrical engineer on a project doesn't have the kind of expertise necessary, a data com consultant is used.

In addition to the connections, piping, pumps, and fixtures of the hot- and cold-water supply and the waste systems within buildings, **plumbing engineers** also deal with circumstances when a site doesn't connect to a municipal water supply and waste disposal: providing water from wells, rivers, springs, or other sources, and disposing of the waste water and effluent through septic systems.

Subspecialists such as *septic* and *hydraulic engineers* may be needed to deal with particularly complex situations.

Other Design Consultants

Lighting design is often performed by specialists known (not surprisingly) as *lighting designers*, whose training is often architectural rather than engineering. Their work is absolutely critical to determining whether the occupants have the proper kind and amount of light to perform their functions well, and whether the architecture looks good or bad, both inside and at night.

Acoustic consultants help design spaces in which sound issues are critical, not only in concert halls and auditoria, where sound travel time, absorption, and reflection and reverberation times are controlled by building shape and materials, but also in other building types, where it may be important to separate the areas that need quiet from the noisier parts of the building (or its systems) and from outside noises. Our firm once designed a school for children with learning disabilities, who were easily distracted by noise. The building had previously been a sports club, and the new design required locating classrooms directly under the gymnasium. Anticipating that noise from structure-borne vibration might create a serious problem, we called in an acoustic engineer, who designed for the gym a new structural slab that floated on a series of huge springs set on neoprene pads on top of the original slab. His solution worked so well that no noise from basketball dribbling or audience cheering reached the classrooms below.

An architect who is not expert at various particular non-engineering parts of a building is well advised to seek a consultant who has specific, current expertise. Among these "architectural trades" are **curtain wall**, **hardware**, **vertical transportation**, and **roofing consultants**. Indeed, there is probably someone out there who knows more than you do about any part of a building. While there is a lot of excellent information to be gained from subcontractors, fabricators, and materials manufacturers, generally more reliable information comes from someone who is not selling you a product. On the other hand, independent information from consultants is not free. (How they are compensated is discussed in chapter 6.)

Speaking of free, since that is one thing buildings never are, architects often need help in knowing what the construction will cost. While most architects feel generally comfortable estimating costs "to a certain degree" of accuracy, if you or your client want assistance in predicting construction costs in more detail, a **cost estimator** does the job. (The architect's role in the determination and responsibility of construction costs is discussed in more detail in chapters 5 and 7.)

Almost every building requires a permit and adherence to local and national codes. In some places and for some large projects, building departments, regulatory agencies, codes, laws, procedures, and the filing, approval, and permitting processes are sufficiently complex and difficult to warrant (or even require) assistance. Consultants variously known as **building department**, **regulatory agency**, or **expediting consultants** provide this help. **Zoning** or **land-use attorneys** may be used as well.

Here are some of the important things you must know to get the most from this sometimes huge cast of characters you are expected to direct and coordinate:

1. **What is needed and when.** Be aware that if you tell consultants too early about some issues they'll waste a lot of time (and probably money) studying them prematurely. If you tell them too late, you will be redesigning your work (and again wasting money) for lacking information when you need it.

2. **Whom you do and do not need.** Determine who is the right consultant within each field for your particular project.

3. **How to organize the project team.** Work out systems for the project's goals, budgets, and schedule, and the flow and format of information: what software, what document size, what drawing conventions.

4. **Which consultants to choose.** Balance new ones, with their knowledge and desire to please new clients (you), with known

consultants whose strengths and weaknesses you know, and with whom you have an existing relationship.

5. *What the work responsibilities, reporting expectations, and liabilities are.* Figure out what chain of command is consistent with your practice and your client's expectations, your consultant agreements, and your liability insurance requirements.

Constructors

It takes a lot of people to commission a project and to design it; it probably takes ten times as many, on average, to build it. The primary party for construction is the ***contractor***. The name derives from the fact that a person or legal entity agrees, by entering into a contract with the owner, to organize, manage, and finance the work and to provide the labor, the materials, the fabricated and manufactured components, and the equipment to produce the constructed, full-scale, fully operational building (or renovation, or addition, or group of buildings, depending on what the project is).

While there are lots of ways to organize the construction of a building project, I will discuss here the traditional format known as ***design-bid-build***. Some of the many alternative processes are described in chapter 4.

In the design-bid-build format, the contactor with whom an owner signs a contract is usually a general contractor, which may be a person or legal entity (such as a privately owned company or corporation, a partnership, or a publicly owned corporation). For simplicity's sake, I will call all of them "company," regardless of which form of organization they are. General contractors arrange, by bidding or negotiation, to provide, for an agreed amount of money, all goods and services necessary to build a project. They usually enter into sub-agreements with other companies, known as subcontractors, to execute portions of the work. While contractors always have foremen and supervisors on their own payroll ("direct staff") and often employ laborers to perform the tasks requiring less skill, such as moving materials, cleaning the work area, and removing debris, all the other trades are normally "subbed out"–that is, provided by various subcontractors. Some general contractors have particular trades on staff: house-building contractors often have carpenters; some subcontractors expand their range by becoming general contractors and keep their subtrade workmen (known as "mechanics," though probably not available to fix your car) on their direct staff. Our firm used a general contracting company run by the son of the founder, who had started the company decades before as a painting subcontracting firm. The son expanded it into a general-contracting business but kept all the original (and subsequent) painters on staff and provided painting services "with his own forces," not through a subcontractor. On large projects even the subs sub out work to firms known as subsubcon-tractors. For example, it is typical, on a medium- to large-size office renovation project, for a general contractor to engage a subcontrac-tor to do the HVAC work. That sub then contracts with one company (also known as "tin-knockers") to sketch, produce, and install the sheet-metal ductwork, another to produce the control systems, anoth-er to install the piping for a radiant heating system, and so on. These companies are all subsubcontractors to the HVAC subcontractor. Further, the HVAC sub probably buys the major HVAC components (boilers, chillers, condensing units, airhandlers, and so on) through an equipment distributor, while each of his subsubs buy their smaller parts on their own.

Suppliers and manufacturers develop, produce, stock, ship, and dis-tribute all the components of a project. Some of these are generic materials, such as wood, which are purchased as commodities by their dimensional and performance specifications and by their price. One rarely demands Lone Star Brand cement, but it is normal to specify paint or light fixtures by brand name because of their design or performance characteristics, which are particular to the manufacturer. Some manufacturers make basically standard products (that is, not highly customized per project), sometimes regularly stocked, but some-times manufactured only when ordered for a specific project. Typically, large and expensive components that can be made with a lot of differ-ent standard options (such as a large HVAC component) or materials ordered in great quantity for a large project are special-ordered.

Fabricators, a kind of supplier, are companies that make, in their shops or factories (but not on site), custom-designed, custom-manu-factured components, such as custom cabinetwork and light fixtures.

The building trades constitute the last group of constructors. Labor unions supply much of the skilled labor employed by the contracting and subcontracting companies mentioned above. Labor unions have training organizations that teach entering workers how to do the job. They provide employee benefits, such as health, welfare, and retire-ment plans, often as multi-employer plans, so that workers can carry their benefits from employer to employer. They bargain collectively with the employer groups and with large contracting companies on compensation, benefits, and work rules. They run hiring halls through which contracting companies can quickly hire experienced, qualified, skilled workers, such as carpenters, masons, or electricians, without doing a lot of time-consuming interviewing and training, thereby mak-ing a more efficient labor market.

Related Fields

While the primary parties—the owners, designers, and constructors—play the central roles in the traditional process of creating buildings, many other individuals and companies play important roles in the enterprise. They can be categorized as those who arrange the money and then the advertising, marketing, renting, and selling of buildings (or potions of them), whom I group in financing, marketing, and sales; and those who control the quality and conformance to laws, comprising research, testing, and public officials. Finally, there are independent project managers, known as owner's reps (representatives), who assist owners lacking the skills or staff to provide all the services required of an owner.

Finance

Because building is expensive, most owners, whether individual homeowners or major corporations, borrow the money to pay for their buildings. The most common form of such borrowing is a *mortgage*, a loan with the property as collateral. For new construction, borrowing typically has two parts: a *construction loan*, which is paid out as the construction progresses, and which is paid off and converted to a *permanent loan*, or mortgage, when the construction is completed. The permanent loan is paid off by the owner over a long period, say fifteen to thirty years.

Here is how the process works. The owner goes to a potential lender, usually a bank, for the permanent loan. The lender receives all the information about the intended building—site information, building plans, owner/contractor contract, financial data on the completed project (also known as a "pro forma") including the costs of operating the property, taxes, insurance, repairs, staffing (if for a commercial property), and how the loan will be paid. For a home, the information includes the income and assets of the homeowner; for a building built by a developer to be rented, the proposed rental structure. The lender analyzes this information and decides whether the project seems to be a good risk, considering the financial soundness of the owner, the borrower, and the value of the project, among other factors. Often banks use a professional *appraiser*, who is qualified to judge the value of a property, to be sure the loan amount is less than the expected/projected value of the completed building. As with a homeowner's mortgage, if the owner doesn't make the monthly payments, the bank will take over ownership of the property. In that case, *foreclosure*, the bank wants to make sure that it will end up owning something worth more than the amount that it lent. Usually the lender requires the owner to put up some personal funds, known as *owner's equity*, to ensure that the *loan-to-value ratio* is less than 1:1, that is, that the property value is greater than the loan, so the property, if foreclosed, wouldn't be "underwater."

If the bank agrees to make the permanent loan, it issues a *commitment letter*, promising to lend the owner the agreed-upon amount upon satisfactory completion of the project. In commercial properties, the required level of completion might go beyond simply finishing the construction and getting a certificate of occupancy—it may even include renting a certain percentage of the space at agreed-upon rents.

The permanent loan answers the issue of how to pay for the finished building, but it doesn't address how to pay for costs incurred before completion, usually including land acquisition, architects' and engineers' fees, and payments to the contractor for construction. To cover these interim costs the owner takes the commitment letter for the permanent loan to a lender, often a different bank, to get the construction loan. The lender for the construction loan runs a higher risk than the permanent lender: What if the construction isn't done right? What if there are cost overruns? What if the contractor disappears or goes bankrupt before the job is done and a more expensive contractor has to be hired to finish the job? What if the owner doesn't manage to sell or rent out the space successfully? The lender of the construction loan needs to spend more time managing. Making sure the payments along the way are in step with the progress of the construction is a very time-consuming task. So the interest rate (the cost of borrowing) is higher for the construction loan than for the permanent loan. This is why an owner who has a construction loan is in a hurry to convert it to permanent financing.

Why, you wonder, am I telling you all this? After all, we're only the architects; let the owners worry about how to get the money! Well, if the owner doesn't get the money, you don't have a project. Further-more, as the architect you will be called on to furnish some of the material to help the owner get the loan, so there is good reason to be well prepared and compelling. Finally, the owner's eagerness to have the building sufficiently complete to convert the construction loan to permanent financing and start making lower monthly loan payments may put pressure on you, the architect, to get the job done. An owner may even "lean on" you to certify completion of work, which could put you in a major liability situation. Interested yet?

Finding mortgage money can be a full-time occupation. Naturally, therefore, it *is* an occupation: ***mortgage brokers*** are hired by owners to help them find funding on the most favorable terms and at the best rates. I mentioned banks as the major sources of money for buildings. Banks are indeed set up to evaluate and process loans. They also used to be the major source of capital to lend. Now there are two other major pools of capital in the United States—pension funds and insurance companies. Their resources add up to trillions of dollars, some of which is used for construction financing. The loans are often administered through banks, but on large projects, money from these sources is often lent directly to owners. Sometimes banks aggregate, or "bundle," groups of mortgages and convert them into securities, known as mortgage-backed securities. Indeed, the world of finance that relates to buildings is as large, as complex, and as fascinating as the world of construction.

Marketing, Sales, and Others

Just as mortgage brokers bridge the gap between the owners and the lenders of the money that enables construction, ***marketing specialists, real estate agents,*** and ***brokers*** make the connection between owners who build buildings for other people and those end users, who may be purchasers or renters, either residential or commercial. Marketing specialists are often involved in projects very early. Our firm once designed an apartment house whose units were to be sold as condominiums. The developer's marketing agent sat in on all the early design meetings, and it became clear that she was the de facto client on all design matters: her opinion on whether a scheme or its features would sell well drove the client's decisions. Marketing agents not only help guide the design but also show the completed spaces, arrange for showings to other brokers to expand the field of sellers, and advertise the project, sometimes using the architect's name as a major selling point (a common strategy, about which one may have mixed feelings).

Owners who do not have the in-house expertise to administer a large construction project may outsource the work to ***owners' reps***, who handle these functions for the owner.

The other groups that have an impact on construction are those that research aspects of construction and of use (far too small an endeavor, in my view) and provide testing services. (There are virtually *no* usergroups/associations that research *uses* of architecture—program, performance, sociology, etc.). Testing of materials and products before they come into the marketplace occurs in many ways to determine their performance characteristics, both under normal use and under stress, such as in fires, earthquakes, floods, hurricanes, or other extreme conditions. This testing, to be credible, should be done by an ***independent testing organization***, either private, such as the Underwriters Laboratory, or governmental, such as the U.S. Bureau of Standards. Because the construction industry and the general public all depend on the standards and specifications published by these groups for buildings' safety and performance, the labs play a critical role. Indeed, many building codes have requirements based on such labs' test results for materials, assemblies of materials, and equipment used in building systems, in relation to fire resistance, smoke toxicity, sound absorption, wearing ability, energy efficiency, and other factors. Independent testing companies also play a role once construction is under way. For example, as concrete is poured on site, samples from each batch and pour are placed in plastic cylinders measuring 6 inches in diameter by 12 inches in length, labeled by date and pour, taken to the lab, and, once they are set, crushed in a machine that measures at what compressive pressure they fail, thereby ensuring (or not) that the concrete from that pour meets the compressive strength that the structural engineer has specified, and upon which the structural integrity of that section of the building relies.

I discuss building and zoning codes in chapter 12, but I will mention here some of the roles that **governmental officials** play in that process. **Zoning and building codes** are researched, proposed and written by governmental officials. After the codes are enacted, building officials *examine* plans for conformance to the laws and *inspect* construction for conformance to the plans that were approved and to the applicable laws and codes. Further, the design, production, inspection, and maintenance of the complex infrastructure of today's world, including roads, mass transit, water supply, waste treatment, and the production and distribution of power, are performed by a wide range of professionals, many of whom do so as government employees.

Federal employees also write and administer laws relating to safety in the workplace, under the Occupational Safety and Health Administration (OSHA), and to accessibility, under the Americans with Disabilities Act (ADA). Some local governments have preservationists and conservationists who work to protect buildings of architectural, historic, or social significance under various landmarks laws. Public health, safety, and welfare are addressed by a wide range of people in public service, as well as by private licensed professionals.

Construction Industry Organizations

All the groups mentioned in this chapter (and thousands more) have organizations—professional, trade, or manufacturing associations—that represent their interests and speak for them. About half the architects in the United States are members of the American Institute of Architects (AIA), which helps represent their interests to the public and fosters professional education and advancement. Engineers have a number of organizations, covering broad ranges of professional engineers (PEs) as well as separate subspecialty disciplines, such as structural or electrical engineers. Planners have the American Planning Association (APA); landscape architects, the American Society of Landscape Architects (ASLA). These organizations of design professionals often work together on public policy and regulatory issues at local, state, and federal levels. Most of the members of these organizations represent small or medium-size firms, and the associations can be powerful platforms for the shared points of view of the individual members. The organizations often write standardized agreements, such as the widely used AIA Documents Series of contracts and forms, which has been in use for almost a century. These are discussed in chapters 5, 6, and 8.

Constructors belong to organizations such as the Association of General Contractors (AGC) and the National Association of Home Builders (NAHB). Most manufacturing groups have associations of their product lines, such as the Architectural Woodworking Institute or the Steel Door Manufacturers Association.

All these organizations, associations, and societies help create profession- and industry-wide standards, raising the quality level and the predictability of the services, the standards of materials, and, ultimately, the quality of the finished product: the buildings.

3 Marketing Architectural Services (Getting the Project)

The great nineteenth-century American architect H. H. Richardson said the three most important things in architecture are "get the project, get the project, get the project." (Every book on architectural practice I've ever read begins with that line. I didn't want to break hallowed tradition, or let you think you weren't reading a real book.) Sadly, he didn't offer much advice on *how* to get the project. This chapter covers a few of the many possibilities I think work.

The most basic approach is to know what you provide best, understand who needs it, and communicate to them your unique ability to provide what they need. Do that in a consistent, organized, focused way and you will have projects.

So, to begin, set goals for yourself and your firm and develop a realistic but optimistic plan—strategy and tactics to achieve those goals.

As I said at the beginning of this book, there are lots of different skills, experiences, talents, and expertise that an architect, whether an individual or a large firm, can have. No architect can be the best at everything for every potential client. So, the first step is to **know yourself**: what you enjoy and want to do, what you have the knack for, and what you have done successfully before and, therefore, have expertise in. You can market aspects of past projects in new combinations. For example, if you've done new science laboratories, renovated old buildings to be offices, and worked on schools that must

be completed and up and running by September 1 without fail, you are probably well suited to convert an old factory into a biotech laboratory that must start operating in nine months or lose its grant funding. You may have never done that exact combination (probably no one has, so don't sweat it), but you should be able to make a persuasive pitch that you are expert at all the parts, so you are absolutely the right architect for BioGenNow's new laboratory project.

Once you have honestly identified your strengths, step two is to **learn about the marketplace**. Identify markets by the obvious factors, including building types, geography, and scale and complexity of project. Delve into the less apparent issues, many of which clients have not articulated and may not even be conscious of. Some clients want trend-setting design that will garner lots of publicity. Some want careful research and thoughtful but modest design that tailors a building to their particular needs. For some clients, the timing of the payment of the architect's fee may be the biggest up-front cost they will have to fund before they get a loan commitment and a construction loan, so the fee, not the quality of the architect's services, is the most important criterion in their selection of an architect. For others, the quality of the design, the inventive use of resources, the assurance of well-produced and thorough construction documents, and the knowledge they will get attentive service are more important than the fee. In fact, fee sensitivity varies tremendously among client types as well as individuals. No chart spells out what clients care about which issues. You only learn it over time and with experience (and sometimes you will be quite surprised). We have had clients for whom the amount of the fee was critical but who seemed indifferent about quality. Others cared about the design, the firm's attention to detail, and the schedule, but openly said that cost was insignificant compared to quality and schedule, or adherence to the budget. The most common and basic characteristic owners look for in design professionals, according to surveys, is **trust**: they want to work with an architect they know will look out for their best interests.

After you have determined what you have to offer and who needs what you've got, you must find a way to let them know. Therefore, step three requires you to **market your services**. You are not selling a small product to a large population, so the traditional methods of mass-marketing through the media, the way some companies hawk beer or breakfast foods, are not the right avenues to reach your potential clients. (And such marketing costs millions of dollars.) So, what is a cost-effective method of reaching your small but unknown target group?

Two media approaches are available: **editorial coverage**–publicity in newspapers, magazines, and broadcast media–and **paid advertising**. Publicity, through media coverage, gives potential clients information about you and your work, at no cost to you. Of course, you can't control getting into the media or what they will say about you. Paid advertising for professional services was prohibited by some states' licensing authorities and considered unethical by professional societies like the AIA (and the American Medical Association and the American Bar Association) until the prohibition was ruled unconstitutional by the Supreme Court in 1977 and a violation of antitrust laws in 1982. Now you can advertise. When tastefully done in a targeted, cost-effective manner, it can be productive. Most advertising by architecture firms appears in small publications, often where the firms' advertising helps to promote the publications' views. Unless you work for a large firm that has an internal "communications," "public relations," or "press" staff or departments, or an outside public relations consultant, it is hard to get your firm's views and projects into the media. But smaller firms can be successful at getting published, especially if they are young and doing adventurous work. Compared to, say, dentists, architects have many opportunities for getting into the news. Some newspapers run articles on residential and commercial design; "shelter" magazines showcase interesting work to a broad audience. The "trade" press–architecture magazines–are often read by sophisticated clients who want to know what's going on.

Then there are the broadcast media. Even if you are not famous enough to be a guest of *The Charlie Rose Show* or *Larry King Live*, whose hosts are avid and knowledgeable interviewers of well-known as well as up-and-coming architects, local television and cable TV stations run stories on local planning initiatives, buildings, and architects. Tune in to these media, get in touch with them, meet and get to know their programmers. If you have a project with unusual ideas or features, point them out. Providing the "hook" for a story can be very productive.

Not many architects get "blind" calls from clients who have read about or seen their projects in the news. But editorial coverage conveys a subconscious seal of approval: the independent selection of your work by the media definitely gives you credibility. Coverage is strong positive reinforcement to clients. Publicity is also a morale booster in an architect's office, particularly if the lead architect shares the credit with the people in the office who did the day-to-day work on a project. Support staff are essential for a project's success (and its newsworthiness).

Today most architecture firms have a *Web site*. Tastefully designed and carefully laid out, a Web site provides at very modest cost a wealth of information about a firm—its personnel, its past projects, and recognition (awards and publications). Even the design of the site itself is a statement about the philosophy of the firm.

Another common way to find work, particularly for firms that are good at doing governmental and large "open bid" private projects, is to respond to publicly advertised *Requests for Proposals,* or *RFPs*, from owners seeking architectural services who list their upcoming projects in various private and governmental publications as well as on Web sites. Architecture firms prepare and submit their qualifications and relevant experience on standardized governmental forms, such as SF 330 (formerly 254–255).

But obtaining media coverage and responding to RFPs only rank number three and four on my list of how to market your services. The absolutely number-one marketing tool is *satisfied clients*. Clients for whom you did a good job, who appreciate and who value your skills, expertise, and efforts on their behalf, are better than any public relations person you could ever hire. Clients who know you cared about them will care about you. They will use you for their next job; they will recommend you to their friends and colleagues; they will provide great references for other potential clients. Keep in touch with former clients, tactfully suggest how they can best maintain and modify what you designed for them, and keep them informed about what you are doing and about recognition and awards you receive. Clients love it (and often feel personal pride) when their architect goes on to greater successes, which can actually enhance the value of their own project. The most successful architecture firms often say that 75 to 85 percent of the work in their offices at any time is for repeat clients.

The second-best method of getting clients is *civic networking*, a technique I learned from my Professional Practice teacher. Senior partner in a large, successful Philadelphia firm, he was from Nebraska; a World War II Navy veteran who had decided he wanted to live in Philadelphia. He knew no one there, but he was a go-getter. He worked for a small firm, got licensed, and joined every civic group he could find: the University of Nebraska's Philadelphia Alumni Society (probably a small group), the Retired U.S. Navy Officers' Club (a bigger group), the local community neighborhood improvement group, church, school volunteer program, and so on. He met a wide range of other civic-minded citizens who saw that he was smart, interested in the community, helpful, diligent, and a hard worker (you *do* have to do more than just join). He soon had a large network of contacts and friends who thought of him when they learned of upcoming building projects. (An advantage of being in a highly specialized profession is that you may be the only architect your friends know!) My professor soon started getting commissions from and through these people, who became satisfied clients. His example alone may have been worth the price of my graduate-school education: I followed it after I graduated and over the years got a lot of work the same way. You should too: it is good for your community as well as for your practice, and it is surprising how often the two go together.

I have left to the end one of the best-known ways for architects to get work: **competitions**. I'll lay my cards on the table right away: I think they are a poor idea in the twenty-first century in the United States, and are an abuse of our profession. (This is probably the topic about which my students disagree with me most noisily, and which provokes the most vocal debates with those rare colleagues who get many of their projects by this means.)

Typically there are two kinds of competitions: *open competitions* that anyone can enter, and *invited competitions*, for which only a small group of architects/firms is asked to submit entries. Often a fee is paid to each invited entrant.

There are pluses to competitions:

1. You get to test yourself on larger projects than you've done on your own.

2. You develop a portfolio of large projects to show potential clients.

3. You may actually win, build a huge project, and become world famous.

However, competitions have downsides, too:

1. You spend a lot of time and money.

2. You design in a relative vacuum, without benefit of productive feedback along the way from an informed client.

3. You waste design in the ecosystem of the design planet. (Why should there be many competition designs that won't get built when there are so many projects built that don't have architect-designed solutions? Eighty-five percent of the construction in this country, it has been estimated, is not designed by architects.)

4. You produce work on behalf of a client who either doesn't pay or underpays for the design. (No firm is ever fully compensated for the time it puts into a competition entry, even in an invited competition. No other profession would do so much free, unpaid, or underpaid work when the prize carries a normal fee. It's like buying a two-dollar lottery ticket with a two-dollar prize.)

5. You are judged as in a beauty pageant—on looks—without regard for your ability to actually do the project.

Would you choose a spouse by viewing candidates on TV and never meeting them to see if the chemistry is good and consider whether a long-term relationship is likely to be successful? I hope not, but isn't that what a competition involves?

My opinion notwithstanding, there are reasonable ways to run competitions. The AIA's guidelines call for clear and impartial rules and fair, independent jury panels. Find out everything you can before you enter a competition. Who is on the jury—do they have a design direction that is different from yours? There are many competitions, not run by AIA standards, that even the most avid, nondiscriminating competition-enterers avoid. If you do enter, you should play to win—and good luck!

However you choose to market your services, follow these pointers:

1. Keep a log of prospects, your actions, and the results.

2. Keep on hand well-designed, current marketing materials—photographs (preferably professionally taken) of completed projects, brochures, a portfolio of projects, a computer projection presentation, and a great Web site.

3. Have a strategy for interviews; practice with a video camera if possible.

4. Research your potential client before the interview, via the Internet, colleagues, and friends.

5. Know the interview setting. You need a different presentation for five people than for fifty.

6. Know the competition. If you are a small firm going up against bigger firms, stress your ability to offer personal attention to an important job. When up against a smaller firm, emphasize the advantages of your firm's depth and horsepower.

7. Emphasize the quality of services you offer rather than your fee structure. Offer to negotiate a fair fee for the project. Avoid being treated as a commodity, where the only (or major) issue is price.

8. Emphasize your unique qualifications for the project.

9. Try to learn the real reason(s) why you fail to get a project for which you were being considered. This is hard: if you get any explanation, it is likely to be more polite than truthful (and helpful).

One of the best books on marketing architectural services wasn't actually written for architects. It is *Confessions of an Advertising Man*, by David Ogilvy, a twentieth-century advertising executive. Out of print, but available in libraries and for purchase secondhand, it is short and a good read. Simply substitute the words "architect" and "architecture" every time he says "ad man" or "advertising." It's great advice for selling your architectural services!

Finally, remember who does the marketing for the firm: *everyone* in your firm. A caller's first impression of your firm is the person who answers the phone the first time. Everyone in the firm makes an impression on clients, potential and current, and must represent the firm in the most professional and courteous manner. The more the staff buys in, the more potential work you'll hear about. Teach your colleagues how to keep their ears to the ground and share their "intelligence," and remember to acknowledge them when the projects are done.

Once you get the knack of going after new business, you will find it is challenging, requires creativity and flair, and, when successful, is very rewarding. Remember: before you can have the fun of doing the project, you have to "get the project, get the project, get the project."

4 Project Delivery Methods

This book concentrates on the classic set of relationships among the three main parties in creating buildings—owner, architect, and contractor. This traditional triad, by which most projects are still done today, operates by what is called the *design-bid-build* method of designing and constructing buildings. In this process (sometimes also known as *design-award-build*), the owner retains an architect to design the project and to prepare plans and specifications (the "design") for several contractors to bid on (the "bid"). The owner then signs an agreement (the "award") with one selected contractor, who builds the project to the plans and specifications prepared by the architect (the "build").

Here I will discuss this arrangement and some alternative methods, as well as some of the many possible variations on those alternatives. There are three parties in the arrangement in every case:

1. A person or group organizes all the aspects of the project and ends up owning the completed work. This person or group defines the needs, finds the site, arranges the financing, and retains, works with, and pays the architect and the builder. I call this party the *owner*.

2. Similarly, the individual or firm (including engineers and consultants) that creates, documents, and manages designs is the *architect*.

3. Finally, the *contractor* comprises the people who carry out the construction of those designs.

Design-Bid-Build

In design-bid-build project delivery, these three separate entities—owner, architect, and contractor—are joined by agreements, with the common goal of a successful project. (Remember: you never have a team where some of the players win and some lose.) But the partners have somewhat differing agendas and economic goals (the money is going to end up in one pocket or another, a natural give-and-take conflict). The separation of owner, architect, and contractor in the design-bid-build process has the advantage that the architect can help protect the owner's interest during construction by monitoring the contractor.

The two primary design-bid-build agreements are the owner/architect agreement, by which the owner retains the architect to provide professional services, and the owner/contractor agreement, by which the owner obtains the construction services, labor, and materials from the contractor to build the project.

When the owner retains one contractor to do all the work, the agreement is a *sole prime general contract* (see fig. 4.1). If the owner has several direct contracts with different contractors for

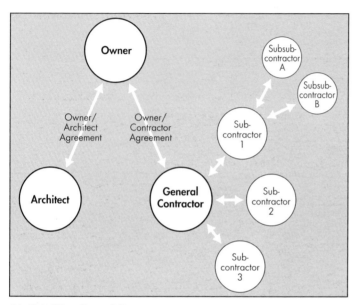

4.1 Sole Prime General Contract

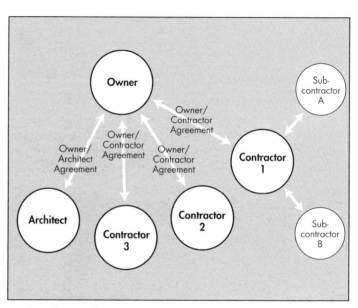

4.2 Multiple Prime Contracts

different parts of the work, they are ***multiple prime contracts*** (see fig. 4.2). "Prime" refers to agreements with the owner, as opposed to agreements between a contractor and a subcontractor. Multiple prime contracts are often used by experienced owners (such as developers and government authorities) who feel that they can manage the construction expertly, thus eliminating the general (sole) prime contractor's overhead and reducing the owner's total construction cost.

The variables are the same in every project:

- **scope of work**, the quantity and quality
- **schedule**—the time it will take to do each portion of the project
- **money**—the cost of each component of the project, including professional fees, the cost of construction, and the cost of borrowing (which is related to time)
- **risk**—how certain it is that the other factors will turn out as expected and desired

There is a great deal of interplay or interrelationship among these factors. For example, if the owner hires a contractor with more skill and more "fat" (spare money to cover the unexpected) in the budget, it will cost the owner more, but the quality is likely to be higher and the schedule is more likely to be met—a trade-off of more money for higher construction quality, more predictability of outcome, and reduced risk.

Before you can recommend a project delivery method to an owner, it is critical to understand the implications of each method for each of the four variables, as well as their hierarchy of importance for the specific owner and project. The owner should specify the order of importance for the project under discussion. The owner can't rate *all* factors equally, because they are never really equal. Some owners are risk-averse and willing to spend extra time or money to achieve the end result with greater certainty. Some must have the best quality and are less sensitive to the cost. Others are very cost-sensitive, with fixed budgets that must not be exceeded. (My first house project was for my uncle—God bless relatives. He said he had $20,000 to build the house—it was the 1960s. I designed a small, simple house, and he hired a good local builder, whom he asked, "How much can you build for the $20,000?" He got the foundations, framing, roof, siding, windows, doors, electrical and plumbing systems, and finished the job himself over the next several years. Kind of like driving up to the pump and saying "Put in $20 worth," rather than saying "Fill'er up.")

A frank discussion of the owner's values and needs will lead to the most appropriate project delivery system.

Construction Management

Construction management is one alternative to design-bid-build. The construction management process still includes three parties, but their roles, responsibilities, and risks are somewhat shifted. In the simplest form, the owner hires a construction manager (CM)—sometimes early in the project, maybe even before selection of the architect—for advice on budget, schedule, and constructability. A good CM has detailed and current information on these issues. When the architect completes the construction documents, the CM puts out bid packages to each trade and levels the bids (a process I describe in chapter 5) and arranges for the owner to sign direct contracts with the building companies, who act here as contractors (see fig. 4.3). The CM is not a direct party to the agreements for the construction work. (In contrast, a general contractor, or GC, contracts with the owner to provide the construction and enters into separate agreements with similar building companies, which then become subcontractors for their portions of the work.) The CM has an agreement only with the owner and, if acting as a *pure CM*, does not sign the agreements with the subs; that is, he "holds" no actual contracts.

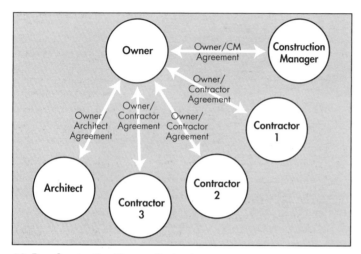

4.3 Pure Construction Manager Contract

The CM provides supervision and management throughout the construction period, providing a professional service at very little economic risk, usually for an overall *fixed fee*, or for a smaller *fixed fee plus* reimbursable expenses, which might include the CM's on-site personnel, such as superintendents and even laborers.

Sometimes, after bidding the various trades to subcontractors, if not acting as a pure CM, the CM, as *agent for the owner*, signs the contracts with the selected subcontractors. A CM may also provide the owner, either at the end of the design development phase or after the construction documents are completed, a *guaranteed maximum price* (GMP) for all the work, limiting the owner's exposure to cost overruns. In contrast to the pure CM, the agent CM takes on a degree of risk. When there is a GMP, the owner may share with the CM any savings resulting from a final cost below the GMP, thereby increasing the CM's incentive to bring the project in under the GMP. (The difference between GMP and final cost is sometimes known as the *saving*.)

Owners view construction management as an advantageous method of project delivery when time is key, because it permits the early trades, such as excavation, foundations, and structure, to begin before the completion of all the other documents, such as the working drawings of the interiors. This makes the project a *fast-track* job. Fast-track projects involve additional liabilities, complexities, and services for the architect, and therefore call for a greater fee.

The CM process is advantageous for very large and complex projects that call for early construction expertise and a reduction in the risks of bidding.

Design-Build

Other common alternative project delivery methods combine two of the three parties into one entity, essentially reducing the parties to two instead of three. In *design-build*, in its purest form, the owner retains one firm that both designs and builds the project, for an agreed-upon sum (see fig. 4.4). Until recently, this has been most

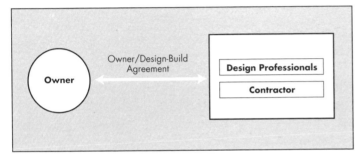

4.4 Design-Build Agreement

commonly used for simple buildings, such as factories and warehous-es, and some kinds of home building. It is gaining popularity with some clients for more complex buildings, including some major gov-ernmental projects. Owners must be able to clearly define their needs and produce very detailed requirements for the building, including size, quality, configuration, and performance requirements regarding daylight, environmental comfort levels, and energy con-sumption. The design-build entity commits to producing a building meeting these requirements for a predetermined cost and on an agreed-upon schedule. Design-build prevents the architect from creating a design that comes in over budget and presumably reduces the economic risk for the owner, but it also eliminates the role of the

architect as representative of the owner's interests by independently monitoring the building process and quality. It also may be harder for the owner to get a satisfactory design because the criteria are simply meeting the original requirements.

A variation on pure design-build is **bridge design-build**. Here the owner hires a "design" architect for schematic design (or even through design development), and the design documents are then given to the modified design-build firm, which prepares the budget and schedule for the project *and* produces the working drawings and specifications (or "technical documents"), just as a fabricator would make a set of shop drawings. The design architect reviews the tech-nical drawings and the construction to help ensure conformance to the design intent and guard the owner's interests. This method is common in Europe and in Japan, where different local traditions or cultural values support the arrangement.

In pure design-build, the relationship between designers and builders is important: who is working for whom? If design is primary, there may be problems of bondability (see chapters 5 and 8) and lia-bilities for the design partner. If contracting is primary, there may be issues about the architect's license and professional liability insur-ance. It is more common and conservative for the contracting to be primary. Architects should consult with their attorneys and insurance carriers before entering any design-build agreements.

Other Methods

Owner-builders have created another project delivery method, in which the owner (usually a developer) is also the constructor, either acting as a general contractor, hiring subcontractors and managing and supervising the work, or acting as the GC *and* providing most or all of the subs—that is, building the project with the owner's "own forces." Owner-builders typically hire architects for the design and construction documents phases, and do the bidding/negotiation and the construction administration themselves. Owner-builders often have very clear design ideas and specifications; their architects provide technical and drafting service rather than creative or management functions.

Possibly the rarest hybrid form of project delivery (so unusual it doesn't even have a common name) might be called the **owner-designer** method. Here the architect also is the owner. Architect John Portman, who designed and owned or co-owned a series of hotels, many with spectacular atrium lobbies, is probably the best-known example.

Many architects have a sideline of building houses on a speculative basis ("on spec"). They act as owner, architect, and builder. Having tried this, I can attest to both the risks and rewards of wearing so many hats.

Construction is an extremely complex endeavor involving many people and risks, both financial and legal. Great fortunes have been made in construction and development (though I haven't heard of any in architecture), so there are potentially substantial rewards as well. Despite the risk factors, which can discourage straying from the status quo, creative new ideas in project delivery methods offer great potential for advancement in construction, an industry that, compared to virtually every other segment of the American economy, is very antiquated, and begs for improvement. In the conclusion I outline some ways architects can lead this change.

5 Owner/Architect Agreements and Architects' Services

This chapter covers the different forms of owner/architect agreements and the phases of services architects provide to owners. Fees are discussed in chapter 6; the other, so-called business terms of an owner/architect agreement are covered in chapter 7. Throughout, the standard for discussion is the garden variety project done by the design-bid-build process, the norm against which I will contrast the variations.

Agreements

General Issues

Reaching the right agreement between the owner and the architect for providing professional services is the most important business part of the profession. Agreements are useful tools to help the parties communicate and to clarify expectations and roles. While many architects and clients focus on fees, the other terms—covering the services to be provided and the responsibilities of each party—usually have greater impact on the success of the project and on the relationship. All parts of the agreement are remarkably interrelated.

An agreement is fundamentally a promise that can be enforced by law. For an agreement to be legal, it must be a mutual assent: two or more parties agree to something, usually the result of one making an offer and the other accepting that offer, for a consideration, usually money. The agreement is a bargained-for exchange of something of value. The parties making and accepting the offer must each do so in a legal capacity: they must be of age and sound mental capacity, and have the authority to enter into the agreement. In an owner/architect agreement, the offerer of professional services must be a licensed architect. Lack of a license can be the grounds for forfeiting fees due! The services offered must be legally permissible and not contrary to statute or common law.

Negotiating the Agreement

Agreements are usually negotiated after the architect has been preliminarily selected. I say "preliminarily" because no selection is final until an agreement is signed. Custom dictates that there be a written agreement, although this is not the way most people retain services from many other professionals (did you ever sign an agreement, other than a waiver, with a doctor?). It is certainly the norm in architectural practice.

Many architects, particularly young ones, hesitate to bargain firmly with their would-be clients for fear of losing the job. But this reluctance may have the reverse effect. You show your savvy by negotiating wisely, fairly, and firmly. Clients size you up during negotiations and wonder, "How will this architect protect my money when dealing with the contractor?" Being too compliant in owner/architect agreement negotiations could well lose you the job. Remember: the goal is to get an agreement that is fair to both sides, for all conceivable situations that may arise during the project.

Forms of Agreement

Depending on the scale of the project, an agreement may be oral (not a good idea, as memory tends to be both self-interested and short), written in a simple letter (for small projects or clients the architect works with regularly), or spelled out in a complex multipage document, either custom-written or a standard form. The standard AIA agreements are useful and have several major advantages. They are revised and updated every decade or so, so they are current with norms and trends in practice and with legal issues. Through a century of use they have been court-tested, and they conform to most states' requirements. They coincide with other AIA agreements used in the construction process, notably the contract between the owner and contractor for construction (discussed in chapter 8), so that all responsibilities, rights, and remedies among the major parties—owner, architect, and contractor—are consistent in the two different agreements that bind the three parties. The AIA B141 Agreement Between Owner and Architect is the most commonly used and is the basis of most other agreements. AIA agreements can be modified to include specifics of the particular project. The forms can be purchased at nominal cost through local AIA chapters or from the AIA in Washington, D.C. They are also available in electronic, editable format from the AIA's Web site by purchasing a license for use. The terms, conditions, and scope-of-services provisions of the AIA agreements are based on the "common trade and practice" of the profession and thus conform to what is reasonable for an architect to do (and not to do). Although the AIA agreements have the AIA name and logo on them, giving the impression that they might favor the architect, they are by and large even-handed, having been written and revised not only by architects but by representatives of contractors' and owners' groups as well.

What are the alternatives to the AIA forms? A simple letter agreement, not uncommon for small projects, stating the scope of services and the compensation can be sufficient, particularly if it references a standard agreement for other terms, notably how problems would be resolved. For more complex projects, a completely custom-written document may be used. Most architects I know would prefer not to spend their time and energy on successfully meeting the criteria outlined above. So architects often rely on their construction (or real estate, *not* general-practice) attorneys to assist in preparing custom agreements.

Finally, and often more dangerous, when a custom agreement is to be used, it is most likely to be a client's standard form. Many large clients—governments, universities, corporations—have their own forms of agreements. These tend not to be as fair to all parties as the AIA forms, which of course is often the very reason why those owners have them. (I once reviewed a large city-agency agreement that in effect provided that all parties agreed in advance that whenever there was a disagreement between the owner and the architect or the owner and the contractor, the owner was correct. What? You don't think that's fair?) Usually these owners give you the choice of using their forms or not working for them. There may be room for negotiation on the topics that architects find most troublesome, depending on how unique (and necessary) are the architect's skills and expertise. How badly the architect wants the project and what level of risk (of uncompensated work or increased liability) the architect is willing to assume are other factors in the decision whether or not to accept the terms, and what fee adjustment should be made for those issues of additional work or risk.

When a client asks for unusual conditions, architects should show the proposed terms to their professional liability insurance company (see chapter 10). An unusual clause may render the architect's insurance void for the project—a result most owners did not intend and do not want. Owners' nonstandard agreements should always be reviewed by the architect's attorney, who should be knowledgeable about construction law.

Services

General Issues

Architects can provide a broad range of professional services for owners. Although sometimes at the beginning of a project the specific services that will be needed cannot be known, to the extent possible the architect and the owner should discuss and agree upon the services that will be provided and the fees the owner will pay for those services. The terms and conditions for each project vary and should be discussed beforehand and clearly stated in the written agreement.

Architects' services, which are discussed in detail in the rest of this chapter, phase by phase, are initially described under the overall umbrella of architects' *general services*, which are provided in every phase—managing and overseeing projects as professional advisors for the owner. Always combining the owners' interests with those of the community and society, in all phases of work the architect does the following:

- administers the project
- consults regularly with the owner
- researches issues
- considers alternatives in design, materials, systems, and equipment

- provides "value-engineering" (how to get the most benefit from every construction dollar to be spent)

- attends meetings

- makes presentations

- issues reports

- prepares and updates project schedules and budgets

- keeps the owners and all other parties fully informed

- submits designs and documents to owners for approval

- assists owners in all governmental and regulatory filings

The importance of communication can't be overstressed. Also, while it is the architect's role to provide professional advice, it is the owner's role to make the business decisions, after receiving the architect's advice.

Owners' responsibilities in normal owner/architect agreements include providing the architect with the *program*, which clearly and fully states the owner's needs, resources, parameters, and goals for the project, and providing all the *site information*. Site information may include a site survey, topographic and utility information, geotechnical data, and any site-specific legal restrictions, such as easements or other encumbrances that would restrict uses or designs that would otherwise be permissible. Sometimes the architect must specifically request needed information and may sometimes write the specification for the survey or other data and arrange for the appropriate professional to provide such data; nevertheless, contractually (and in common practice) the data are provided by the owner, and the architect has the right to rely on the accuracy and completeness of those data.

For the project to go smoothly, there are other *owner's obligations* that must be also met. They must answer questions from the architect in a timely manner and stick to decisions they have made. Owners must pay the architect amounts due for professional services and for reimbursable expenses, when due, as specified in the agreement. Should the owner fail to perform these obligations, the project will not meet the owner's schedule or budget, and the architect may be entitled to additional compensation.

Once an agreement is reached, the first task of an architect is to evaluate the proposed program, budget, schedule, site, and method of contracting for construction services, to see that they all fit together and are realistic. Experience and good judgment must prevail over sheer optimism; if the schedule is too short or the budget is too low for the necessary scope of work (I've rarely heard of a budget being too high), it is time to tell the owner and deal with it together to make the pieces fit *before* design work begins.

Next the architect assembles the team for the project, selecting the appropriate consultants, negotiating the fees for their services, reviewing with the owner the proposed list of consultants (such as structural engineers, MEPS engineers, acoustic consultants). There's no sense engaging a consultant the owner distrusts or is suing on another project. Show consultants the terms of your agreement with the owner; they must be bound by the same terms. Review the goals, scope, budget, and schedule of the project with all the consultants. Review their professional liability insurance coverage. Sign the agreements with the consultants.

Five phases of architects' work constitute, in most architect/owner agreements, what are now often defined as **standard services** (formerly called **basic services**). These must be considered in discussion of compensation and of what services an architect can undertake beyond standard services, which become **changes in services** (formerly called **additional services**), for which an owner may be obligated to pay additional fees. (Got your attention? More on fees in chapter 6.) The general services described above apply to each of the five phases of services, which include three design phases: schematic design, design development, and construction documents. These traditionally have been clearly delineated and distinct stages; their boundaries today are somewhat blurred by the use of CAD and alternative project delivery methods. The three phases now tend to be more evolutionary than separate. Moreover, new services that architects can provide (often for additional fees), such as energy audits, sustainable design considerations, security design, and concerns about indoor air quality, need to be addressed in all phases.

Schematic Design

The purpose of schematic design is to develop an approach, an idea, a *parti* that synthesizes all the information about the client and the site into an arrangement of spaces that responds to all the issues, meets all the requirements, and can be refined into a wonderful building. Simple, no?

You have a signed agreement; you have the client's program and you understand it. You have spoken at length with the client and with all the related groups or subgroups you and the client think are relevant. You know not only the specific requirements of spaces and adjacencies but also the client's goals and aspirations (both explicit and unspoken), as well as the time and budget allowed. You have done preliminary research, which usually includes gathering independent information about the client and the project type and examples of the project type (bad examples can be just as illuminating as good ones). You know the site's legal constraints (both site-specific, such as easements, and general, such as the requirements of zoning and other governmental entities that have jurisdiction). You have surveys showing boundaries, topography, utilities, and other critical site features; you know the history of and future plans for the site and surrounding sites, as well as data about climate, solar orientation, and surrounding sites; you have aerial photos and (if the project is an alteration or addition to an existing building) measured drawings. You have walked the site and gotten to know it at different times of day and from different vantage points, both good and bad. You understand its character and potentials. You have checked the potential for natural disasters, such as floods, earthquakes, forest fires, tornadoes, and hurricanes. And last but not least, you know the potentials and limitations of the locally available construction forces.

You now have a lot of information and the proverbial "blank page." How to begin? This moment is simultaneously exhilarating and frightening; most architects gradually develop personal strategies that work for them, help reduce fear, and lead toward solutions.

The appropriate process or strategy obviously is related to the scale and type of project as well as what is best for each architect's personal (or corporate) working method. A small house can be designed with a more intuitive, subjective approach; a large, complex building requires a more orderly, analytic approach. The design at this embryonic stage shows the scale and relationship of the project components—the plan for the building relative to the site, its solar orientation, and views; it presages what the building will be like spatially and architecturally.

From the intuitive end of the spectrum of methods, some architects simply start sketching, in plan and in three dimensions, to see where it will lead, slowly molding these sketch ideas into plans, section, and massing. (I once shared offices with an architect who actually begins with a large lump of modeling clay and molds it into different shapes until he finds one that satisfies his very well informed artistic sensibilities.) More objective designers graphically define the site in terms of setbacks, views, sun angles, prevailing winds, access, and formal "regulating lines," building up these layers into an informed site plan, often in a personal diagrammatic style. They put the program information first into accurately scaled blocks, then arrange and rearrange the blocks to meet the adjacency requirements most optimally, until a plan begins to appear. They then insert this on the site plan and adjust it to adapt to the site parameters, until they develop a plan that is fully related to both the client's needs and the potentials and restrictions of the site.

Whatever way suits you and the particular project, the next step is to present it to the client. There are many ways to do this. Some architects like to show the client a fully developed schematic design with final drawings and perhaps a model, with an explanation of how they developed it and what the benefits of the scheme are. Others feel more comfortable letting the client be more of a participant in the evolution of the scheme, showing the client several alternative approaches at each step of its development, discussing the pros and cons of each variation, getting the client's feedback and incorporating it in the process, and ending the schematic design phase with a scheme the client participated in forming. There is rarely only one way to solve a problem, and the client is often very useful in narrowing the alternatives to the best and most suitable direction.

No one method is right or wrong. Each has its advantages and pitfalls. Ultimately the best choice for a specific combination of architect, client, and project depends on chemistry, history, and personal style. I prefer the cooperative process because clients rightfully feel more positive about schemes that they help shape, schemes that benefit from their knowledge of the program's subtle implications. (Better that *they* make those adjustments along the way than *you*.)

When you prepare a presentation for a client, remember that the central objective is to communicate your ideas so the client can fully understand (and appreciate) your concept. Why do I need to say this? Sometimes architects view presentations as a chance to show the client how clever they are (the implication being, perhaps, how much *more* clever than the client—probably not true, and pointless in any event) and devise tricky presentations that have the effect of concealing their ideas rather than explaining them. While some sophisticated clients can read drawings as well as architects, most clients cannot. Plans, elevations, and sections are abstractions, a language that must be learned; no one is born knowing it, though some grasp it faster than others. Perspectives are easier for most lay people to understand. Your clients may be very smart (remember: they hired you), but your drawings are unfamiliar territory.

I know a conductor who can look at a musical score, hear the sounds it represents, and know if it will sound good or not. To me, a score is a nice graphic interplay of horizontal lines and dots with tails. I am like a client for whom we once designed a house: he seemed very pleased with the design and at the signing of the construction contract said he couldn't wait for the work to begin. He did express one reservation, though: he wasn't sure that he was going to like so many round things all over the house. I was baffled until he pointed to a door swing, and I realized he didn't have a clue what we'd been showing him all those months or what the house was going to be like. (The ending was happy: he lived there with his family for over twenty years and did not miss having a lot of round things in every room.)

If your clients don't understand the drawings you show them, you are not communicating successfully and you are not doing your job right. And when there is a gap between expectations and reality, it usually leads to a problem.

Your schematic design work should always be one scale ahead of what you present to the client. By this I mean that if you show a client a scheme at 1/8" = 1'-0", make sure you've already worked it out at 1/4" scale. This way you won't "sell" something you can't resolve in more detail as you move forward.

When you show a scheme (or multiple schemes, if you see alternate ways of solving a problem and want the client's guidance on the choices), be sure to get clear instructions about where your first schemes are lacking before you go back to rethink and redesign. If a client says "I don't know why, but this doesn't work for me," you don't have enough information to make your next effort meaningful. You are into guessing territory, which can only end in frustration. We once showed a client three designs for a grand stair. He said the designs were very interesting, but there must be other ways of doing it. Of course there were other ways—many of them! But we had already looked at and discarded about a hundred. We came back several weeks later with six more stair designs. "Well," he said, "that proves your first three were the best!" Gee, thanks. Get the client to make specific, constructive suggestions. Take notes and issue minutes of the meeting to record what the deficiencies were and what were the agreed-upon remedies. Resolving open issues at every stage is critical. When clients don't have schedules to meet, you can waste a lot of time, and even a large fee can disappear very fast.

To complete the schematic design phase, you must do three more things:

1. *Prepare an outline specification*, also known as a ***scope of work***. In it you list every section of work to be carried out, typically in standard Construction Specification Institute (CSI) format (discussed later in this chapter). These sections might include Earthwork, Foundations, Structure, Finishes, Mechanical Systems, and so on, as relevant for the project. Depending on the scale of the project, the outline spec may take from several pages to several hundred pages to itemize. It should describe briefly, in writing, the components of the project—what kinds of systems, materials, and so on you intend to use. At this stage you don't need model numbers or methods of fabrication, just general descriptions.

2. *Review the project schedule* you prepared at the beginning of your work and revise if it has changed at all. Beware of promising, "It's okay that Schematic Design took so much longer than we originally planned; we'll make up the time in the next phases." Lost time is rarely found. Be realistic.

3. *Prepare a statement of probable cost*. This, like all cost estimates prepared at each stage of work, is not a guarantee of the final cost but a statement of what, in your best judgment, the cost of the project is likely to be. It is based on the degree of specificity of the information developed so far. At the completion of schematic design you will most likely prepare this estimate based on ***unit costs***—for example, the project is x square feet (or cubic feet, depending on the building type) and for this building type, at this time, in this place, at the intended level of quality and complexity, you estimate a cost of y dollars per unit. So the construction cost will likely be x units times

y/unit. (A surprising number of people tell me they would have gone into architecture except for the math. This is about the toughest math most architects do.) Then you add a percentage for **escalation** (how much you expect the cost to increase, through market inflation, between the time of your first unit-cost-basis estimate and the expected construction date), a percentage for **design contingency** (the "improvements" that often creep into a project between schematic design and the final construction documents that go out to bid), a percentage increase for **bidding contingency** (the uncertainty of the marketplace), and a percentage increase for **construction contingency** (unforeseen site or field conditions, and inadvertent omissions that need to be added to finish the job properly). Construction contingency does *not* cover client-initiated changes—those are unpredictable and incalculable. (If the client promises to make no changes, there will be no costs, so it won't be a problem.)

When the client has agreed to the design, the outline spec, the schedule update, and the statement of probable cost, you get the client to sign two sets of the drawings on which you have stamped "This Schematic Design is approved by the undersigned, and the architect is authorized to proceed to Design Development." The client keeps a signed set and you keep a signed set. These drawings, specs, schedule, and budget answer questions later about what was agreed about standard (or basic) services. They are your "approved drawings" at this stage. You are ready to proceed to the next phase of work.

Design Development

The goal of design development is to refine the design prepared in the schematic design phase so that every design decision necessary to build the project is considered, revised if necessary, and confirmed. In an ideal world (a place, sadly, I've never found), at the end of design development you should be able to go off and produce the construction documents without ever having questions for the client. While this may not happen in real life, it should be a goal. Design development is the time to focus on the complex interplay of all building parts—architectural, structural, mechanical, electrical, plumbing, and sprinkler. All the building systems must be designed completely enough so all the architectural implications of each part of the building designed and provided by consultants (column and beam sizes, duct sizes, chase sizes, mechanical-room sizes and locations, and the like) are known to you so you can produce construction documents that don't require constant modifications. It's enough work to do them well once; try not to do them more! Now is also the time to review the zoning and building codes as they relate to every aspect of the project, to be as sure as possible that your design conforms.

Once the design development decisions have been honed and set, you will do the same three things you did in schematic design, but in more detail: prepare an outline specification; revise, if necessary, the project schedule; revise the statement of probable cost. This time the statement of probable cost is based on more detailed take-offs and prices done either by your own staff or with an outside cost consultant (sometimes called an estimator), or by a contractor. Carefully review any statement prepared by an outside consultant. It's amazing how often estimators get exact right prices for things that aren't even in the project. Finally, you get the client to sign the design development drawings, specifications, schedule, and budget, authorizing you to proceed to the next phase, construction documents.

Construction Documents

The preparation of construction documents is the biggest phase of an architect's work, commanding the largest part of the fee and the most time and effort to execute. The construction documents are two-part: the visual, graphic portion known as the **working drawings** and the verbal, text portion, accurately called the **project manual** but incorrectly (and most commonly) known as the **specifications**, or **specs**. It is helpful to understand exactly the purposes of the construction documents. They describe clearly and precisely what is to be built, like a giant set of instructions for the contractor, and they become the central part of the contract between the owner and the contractor. Construction documents state exactly what is the scope and quality of work the owner is purchasing from the contractor for a sum of money to be specified. These documents are also the major components of the contract documents (see chapter 8).

Working Drawings

The working drawings communicate a vast amount of information as thoroughly and as succinctly as possible. Preparing a good set takes experience, thoughtfulness, and planning. In our office we begin with a "cartoon" set, in which we sketch on 8 ½" x 11" sheets the content, scale, and layout of each final drawing. We then begin the drawings and build them up one by one. Often the starting point is simply the CAD drawings from earlier phases, reorganized and with added information, such as dimensions, notes, and cross references (keys) to other drawings.

Learning how to do a good set of working drawings is an important part of an architect's training and usually is a segment of an internship. Ask questions and spend as much time as you can studying what your office considers good sets of drawings for previous jobs. Such model sets of drawings, from your employers, friends, mentors, or teachers, as well as in books, are valuable resources. A good architect spends a lifetime honing these skills, because the quality of your working drawings becomes the quality of your buildings. Most firms develop consistent office standards for directories, file naming, layering, drawing-set organization, dimensioning, text and graphic standards, and the keying of drawings to each other so there is consistency from project to project, and not constant reinvention of the wheel.

Traditionally the drawing order is by discipline: architectural, structural, mechanical, electrical, plumbing, and sprinkler. Within each discipline the traditional (and expected) order is: plans, elevations, sections, and details, going from the most general to the most specific. Why is it useful to follow this order rather than being inventive and more creative? Remember the purpose: if you make it easy for contractors to understand the information quickly and in a way with which they are familiar (that is, the conventional order), you are more likely to get lower bids and hence to build more of your designs to the highest quality possible. Young architects have suggested to me that showing the first-floor architectural plan, then the first-floor structural plan, then the first-floor mechanical plan, then the second-floor architectural plan, the second-floor structural plan, and so on, is a logical sequence, but this order makes it very hard for the subcontractors who are bidding and building to find the information in which they are interested. The mechanical subcontractor doesn't really care a lot about the structural work, and it would be inefficient, annoying, and eventually costly to the client if that subcontractor has to try to find his mechanical drawings as every fifth drawing in the set.

Project Manual: Front End

Because the project manual includes two types of information, it is divided, conceptually, into two parts. The first, informally known as the *front end*, includes all the business parts of the agreement and the conditions of the relationships of the parties. It may include, in the standard design-bid-build arrangement, the following eleven items.

1. The *Invitation to Bid Letter* invites each contractor to submit a bid on the project and describes the project in general terms; how many sets of bidding documents are provided and how to obtain additional sets; the bid due date, location, and whether the bids will be opened publicly or privately; whom (typically in the architect's office) to contact for information and to arrange a site visit; and any other special information about the bid process or the project. Public (governmental) projects usually require that the contract be awarded to the lowest qualified bidder. In projects where this is not a requirement, the invitation to bid should state that the owner may reject a bid for any (or no) reason. This proviso permits the owner to select a bidder other than the low bidder, perhaps one whose bid is only slightly higher than the low bidder, about whom you might have some qualms. The proviso may cause some potential bidders to decide not to take the time to prepare a bid. In fairness, everyone should know in advance what the process will be.

2. The *Instructions to Bidders* may be either a standard form (such as the AIA A-701 document) or the owner's or architect's own form, customized for the project. The instructions inform bidders of their obligations to carefully review all the contract documents and all the conditions (market, site, and so on) under which they will be expected to do the work, and of their obligation to sign a contract based on their bid, should it be accepted.

3. The *Bid Form* contains spaces for the bidder to fill in its name; its bid for the overall contract sum; a breakdown of the contract sum for each trade, for general conditions, and for overhead and profit; a completed unit price list (see #7 below); prices for each alternate (see #8 below); the cost of any bonds required; the time to mobilize and begin the work, and the period to execute the work. It must be signed by an officer of the contracting company and carry the corporate seal.

4. The *Form of Contract*, whether a standard one such as the AIA A-101 or a customized one, is included; it is filled in and signed later, when the contractor has been selected. It includes the owner's and contractor's names and addresses, the full list of the contract documents with their dates, the terms, and the price, known as the *contract sum*.

5. The *General Conditions of the Contract* are the rules of the road for the prosecution of the work. The AIA A-201 offers one version; some owners and architects prefer to use their own. The document describes what each party is to do and spells out the remedies should any party fail in its obligations. (This topic is covered at length in chapters 8–10. There are a lot of issues here.)

6. The *Supplementary Conditions* (formerly, and more descriptively, known as the Supplementary Conditions of the General Conditions of the Contract, an absurdly long name) change certain provisions of the General Conditions of the Contract. The supplementary conditions are sometimes called *riders*. They itemize additions, deletions, and modifications, by paragraph, section, and line, to the AIA A-201 or whatever version of General Conditions is being used in order to adapt to an architect's preferences of details of practice or to fit the particulars of the project.

7. A list of *Unit Prices* contractors are asked to bid on. The major portions of most buildings are composed of very few different components. In order to determine fairly the value of any changes made to the project during the construction process, it is helpful to agree in advance, by including a list of prices, what it costs to add or subtract different quantities of these components. Thus the list might include "$x per cubic yard for poured-in-place concrete," or "$y per outlet for an electrical duplex convenience outlet," or "$z per linear foot for an 8'-0" high partition Type A (as shown on the drawings) gypsum drywall partition and studs." Unit prices typically include the material, labor, shipping, tax, overhead, profit, and all other costs associated with the item. Having a carefully chosen list of unit prices reduces causes for disputes between the contractor and the owner during construction and avoids unnecessary friction if and when changes are made.

8. *Alternates* are possible changes to the basic work shown in the construction documents; alternates describe either the addition or subtraction of a chunk of work, or the substitution of one kind of work for another. For example, an alternate might specify the savings in "eliminating the Northern Wing of the building" or "the cost of adding the millwork shown in Drawing Alternate #3." Or it might specify, "In room #36 in lieu of (or in exchange for) the vinyl-composition-tile resilient flooring specified in the Finish Schedule on Drawing A-27, furnish and install Tenderfoot EZ Care carpet, as manufactured by XYZ Carpet Co, Anytown, North Carolina, on rubberized padding." Or, "In First Floor Auditorium, area #1009, in lieu of specified wall coverings, provide paint, System 9, per specifications." Alternates, the prices of which are furnished as part of and at the same time as the contractor's formal bid, are ways of adjusting the bid price to meet an owner's budget. Rather than spend a long time negotiating after the bids come in, the owner can quickly decide upon the final scope of the work to be contracted for, and rapidly achieve the budgetary goal.

9. *Allowances* are provisions for items that haven't been designed yet or that can't be known at the time the agreement is signed. For example, if you are building a large corporate headquarters on a tight schedule and all the documents are complete except for the selection of finishes, such as the wall coverings in the executive board room, the agreement may specify, "Allow $5,000 for the purchase of wall covering material for room #1325. The shipping and installation shall be carried separately in the base bid." When wall covering is finally selected, if it costs $3,000 the total contract sum is adjusted down by $2,000. Another reason to carry an allowance is for the unknowable. Excavation may require unforeseen blasting or jack-hammering to remove rocks larger than a laborer can lift. You can set a unit price per cubic yard and carry an allowance for, say, $20,000 for rock removal. Again, the contract sum is adjusted when the exact cost is known.

10. *Phasing Requirements* need to be stated if the project cannot be built in the normal way, as one continuous process. For example, if work is to be done in a building that is partially occupied by users, the contractor must build in several stages. This takes longer and costs the contractor more—in supervisory time, in the number of subcontractors' callbacks to be arranged, in rental costs for job-specific equipment, and so on. The contractors must include these additional costs in their bids. (It costs the owner much more if the owner tells the contractor later.)

11. *General Notes* are the last part of the front end of the project manual and a natural segue into the technical sections. The General

Notes comprise instructions to the contractor and the subcontractors about issues that apply to every trade, but that are easier to say once than to repeat at the beginning of every section. For example, a note may warn each trade that by beginning work it is accepting the work of the previous trade and will be held responsible for meeting the requirements of its section even if it was not possible to do so because of a deficiency in the prior work. For example, say a painter comes to the job site to paint a plaster wall and sees that the wall was badly plastered. The painter can (1) perform sanding and patching work beyond normal painting preparation; (2) paint the wall as is and end up with an unsatisfactory paint job that doesn't meet the paint specification requirements for uniformity of finish; or (3) advise the general contractor that the previous work, the plastering, was not properly done, and painting will not begin. In choice #1, the painter must either unfairly absorb the additional cost of fixing someone else's bad work or ask the contractor for additional money to do the extra work. (If the contractor agrees, this amounts to choice #3.) In choice #2, if the painter does the work on the bad wall, he has "bought" the precondition and will not be paid for his unsatisfactory painting work. In choice #3, the correct choice spelled out in General Notes, the contractor either gets the plasterer back to fix his work or pays the painter an additional fee (to be agreed upon before the extra work is done, if the painter expects to be paid for it). The General Notes try to put every trade on notice about conditions and requirements that apply to all trades on a job.

Project Manual: Technical Sections

The second part of the project manual comprises the **technical sections**, or specs. (This is why the whole book is not accurately called the specs.) The technical sections, which describe each type of work, or trade, are always in the same order, following the uniform, industry-wide norm; it is the order followed by the Construction Specification Institute (CSI), Sweet's catalogs, and every other compendium of building-parts information. Doors and Windows are always in Section 8. Gypsum Drywall, Painting, and Carpet are always subsections in the Finishes part, Section 9. Every section is divided into similarly standard subsections. This standardization allows everyone always to find information in the expected places. The order of the sections is from the simplest, least fabricated components, such as earthwork and concrete, to the more complex and highly fabricated components, such as HVAC chillers and emergency generator systems.

There are two basic ways to specify work. The **prescriptive method** describes exactly what materials and format the work will be done with; the **performance method** describes the final results that must be achieved. A prescriptive painting spec might say, "Apply two finish coats"; a performance spec, "Apply as many coats as necessary to achieve a uniform coat." If the painters can make a surface uniform in one coat, they've satisfied the performance requirement; if it takes them ten coats to make it uniform, there is no extra charge. A prescriptive spec for air conditioning might spell out all the equipment, the ductwork sizes and locations, and so on. A performance spec might say, "When it is 90 degrees outside, the system will maintain an indoor temperature of 72 degrees, at 50 percent relative humidity, at an energy consumption not to exceed x watts per square foot and at a noise level no greater than y decibels."

Technical sections include the following parts:

- scope
- related work
- reference standards
- submittals
- warranties and guarantees
- products
- labor
- execution

Technical sections often outline the scope of work covered by the section (perhaps by listing the locations in which the work occurs, which helps the subs bidding the job find the work for them to bid on); the related work (for example, the painter should want to read the plastering spec to know the quality level the plasterer must achieve); relevant reference standards that must be met (some industry and trade organizations write their own standards for trades and products, often volumes of them, which can be included by reference, an easier and more succinct procedure than repeating them); and the materials to be used (listed by manufacturer, make, and model or by type and quality). Many technical sections require *submittals* before the subs order or make the actual products or materials. Submittals can include *shop drawings* (detailed drawings prepared by the subs who fabricate all the custom-made portions of the job, such as cabinetwork and ductwork, which show the exact dimensions, materials, and methods of joining and installation); physical *samples* of the materials (for example, from the actual quarry section or slab for stone, the mill run for dyed carpet); *schedules* listing the details of materials and products to be used in each location (for example, door and hardware schedules, which list exact sizes, types, pieces, and functions for every door); and *cuts*, which are catalog or product descriptions listing all the relevant specifications, to ensure that the project requirements are met. Submittals allow the architect to check the contractor's conformance to the specifications and, most important, the design intent. While they are necessary ingredients for well-built buildings, submittals cost contractors money to prepare, obtain, deliver, track, and resubmit if required. So, if you expect contractors to prepare submittals, you must spell out in detail in the specs what your requirements will be so the costs of providing submittals can be included in their bids.

Standard construction as defined in the AIA A-201 General Conditions comes with a one-year warranty from the contractor. If there are any portions of work for which it would be appropriate or desirable to have a longer **warranty** or **guarantee** (such as roofs and air-conditioning compressors), that requirement must specified in the relevant technical section, including how long the warranty or guarantee is for and who backs it up. I would rather have a national insurance company behind a thirty-year roof guarantee than a lifetime warranty from Joe's Quick and Ready Back-of-the-Truck Roof Repair Company. (A warranty covers services or products of the party making the warranty; a guarantee is made by one party for goods and services of another party. For example, a contractor provides a warranty for its own work; an insurance company provides a guarantee for the contractor's work. The distinction between these terms is often lost in real life, and they are usually mistakenly used interchangeably.)

In the technical sections of a project manual, **products** are defined by manufacturer and model as well as requisite components and accessories.

Labor for certain kinds of work must be specially trained and have experience in installing special kinds of systems, such as specialty roofing products. If the technical section specifies that the roofs be installed only by mechanics trained (or even certified) by the manufacturer, with a certain number of years' experience installing those roofs in that area on those building types, you should expect to get it; if you don't specify it, you probably won't. And it's very hard to ask for it after the work begins.

Execution describes the necessary site conditions (such as temperature and humidity) under which work must be done, necessary preparation, and the remedies of reinstallation, adjustment, or cleaning to correct any deficiencies. If work must be tested after installation in order to ensure conformance to the specification requirements, you must specify the requisite testing—by whom, when, what tests, and what the remedy is if the work fails the tests. Finally, any required owner interface about start-up or "commissioning" would be covered.

The architect and the owner have every right to get everything the specifications require the contractor to provide, do, not do, and so on. What is not fair (and what contractors probably won't do without extra charge) is to ask for more to be done after the contract is signed.

Project manuals vary in length from a brief booklet to multivolume sets of hefty books. The thoroughness (and bulk) of the project manual should be appropriate to the size and complexity of the project.

Bidding and Negotiation

When construction documents are complete and have been reviewed and approved by the owner, you are ready to put them "out to bid" to a number of contractors, or to negotiate a contract with one contractor. The method of contractor selection depends on the owner's preference or legal obligations. If the owner is a governmental entity, **open bidding** may be required—advertising the bid process and offering it in a public process to any contractor meeting the statutory requirements. Private owners usually elect **closed bidding**—creating a list of qualified, appropriate bidders and putting the project out to bid with them. Experienced owners often compile their own list of bidders, sometimes from a stable of contractors whom they already know. Less knowledgeable owners may need assistance from the architect in developing a good bid list of suitable contractors.

The issues to consider in assisting an owner in contractor selection are the contractor's experience at the particular building type, at the scale of project, and in the geographic area as well as the contractor's reputation. Is the contractor known for delivering quality and timely work? For accurately adhering to the requirements of contract documents? For identifying potential problems in advance? A contractor who calls the architect to warn that if he or she is not on site in fifteen minutes the job will grind to a halt because there is a problem that needs an immediate answer is not one who plans ahead. And a contractor known as a wild or obnoxious "extra" hunter is obviously one to avoid.

If you know contractors who meet the criteria for the particular project, put them on the bid list. If you don't, some research is in order. Ask other architects whose judgment you trust and who have done similar projects. Look around the area at recently built similar projects, find the owner and architect, and ask for recommendations. Look in publications for similar projects, and contact the architects.

Once you have a preliminary list, interview the architects of each contractor's projects and ask your client to contact the owners they worked for. Architects and owners provide different kinds of information; with information from both, you should have a good start on a short list of bidders. Then, with the owner and relevant consultants, interview these potential bidders. With the owner, visit recent projects that are similar to the proposed project in scope, quality, and building type. Seeing the actual work is different from looking at photos. After interviews and site visits, compare your notes and impressions with the owner's and check references. This work will produce the final bid list of qualified contractors acceptable to both you and the owner. Be warned that even with the most carefully prepared list, past results are not an ironclad guarantee of future performance. Our firm has used contractors who did one (or several) projects competently and then really messed up. A change in personnel or bad chemistry with the client can make the difference.

The alternative to bidding a project is to negotiate a contract with a contractor selected by agreement of the owner and the architect. This process offers the advantages of knowing what you are getting and saving time. Sometimes owners bring a preferred contractor in early (sometimes even before the architect starts) to assist in scheduling, budgeting, and reviewing the design and materials for constructability. While preselection is advantageous on those issues, the cost savings of competitive bidding is lost. Whatever the procedure, the architect's job is to inform the owner thoroughly; the owner's job is to make business decisions that balance risk and reward for the owner.

Once a bid list is assembled, the architect assists the owner in soliciting bids, usually by advising the bidders before sending them the bidding documents, and confirming their interest and ability to meet the bid schedule. The architect sends an agreed-upon number of sets of bidding documents, including working drawings and project manuals, and additional copies of the bid forms to each bidder simultaneously so that all bidders receive the same information at the same time.

During the **bid period**, the time between sending the bidding documents to the bidders and when the bids are due, the architect helps arrange site visits for contractors and subcontractors (usually keeping a log of visitors, with names and dates) and answers the questions that inevitably arise as contractors study the bid documents. A good format is to have all questions sent in writing to the architect, who then periodically prepares answers, called **bid addenda**, which are first reviewed by the owner and then faxed or e-mailed to all the bidders at the same time. Even if a bidder didn't ask a question, each bidder deserves to hear every question and every answer. Other bid addenda consist of additional information developed by the architect after the documents are sent out to bid. Since these addenda become an integral part of the contract for construction, they must be prepared with the same care, clarity, and accuracy as the rest of the documents. Each bid addendum should have a number and date, for future reference.

Bids must be submitted by the required date. They are date- and time-stamped on receipt and opened by the owner and the architect together, either with the contractors present ("publicly") or not ("privately") as the Invitation to Bid letter specified. It's a good idea for owner and architect to sign each page upon opening a bid, to record that it was the actual page received by the deadline and at the opening. Because bid tampering is a potential cause of legal action, it is important to follow these steps rigorously, to ensure both the appearance and the fact of propriety—that the bid process was carried out fairly and competitively.

Once the bids are opened, the architect prepares a **bid summary**, a spreadsheet tabulating the bidders; contract sums, trade breakdowns, costs for unit price items, alternates, bond costs, and dates for starting and completing the work. The architect assists the owner in "leveling" the bids—looking for anomalies and making sure all bids are comparable. Then the owner can select on a low-bid or other basis, as specified in the Invitation to Bid letter. The winner is notified, and the losing contractors should be too. Too often, contractors who went to the effort and substantial expense of preparing a bid never hear anything back. Architects, who sometimes suffer the same discourtesy, should avoid it.

How do you ensure that the winning contractor will sign a contract for the bid amount rather than walk away? There are two ways, either of which must be required by the bid documents. With a **bid bond**, which a contractor obtains from an insurance company and submits with the bid, an insurance company in effect guarantees that if the contractor doesn't enter into an agreement with the owner for the bid amount, the insurance company will make up the difference between the contractor's bid and that of the next lowest bidder by paying the owner the difference (and probably never insuring that contractor again). With a **bid security**, the contractor submits a certified check for a specified dollar amount or percentage of the bid, along with the bid. If the contractor fails to enter into an agreement with the owner

for the bid amount, the security is forfeited to the owner. Either method is a fairly strong disincentive for a contractor to "walk."

Contract Administration

The contract administration phase typically makes up 20 percent of the architect's fee, yet the description of this phase in most owner/architect agreements is longer than that of all the other phases together. Probably because it involves a third party (the contractor), it is the phase when most problems occur, and it takes the architect's greatest expertise (and diplomacy) to accomplish smoothly.

After the owner/contractor agreement has been signed, the architect's role subtly shifts. Now the architect must act not only as the owner's professional advisor but also as an even-handed administrator of the construction contract, showing favoritism to neither the owner nor the contractor. Many owners expect the architect to be their advocate in this phase. While a lawyer may serve in this capacity, an architect should not. Contractors rely on the architect's fairness and enter into the owner/contractor agreement on that basis. An architect who favors the owner hurts the contractor economically. Not only is a biased architect unethical, but when other contractors learn of it (there are no secrets in the construction world, after all), they will provide for it in future bids with the architect by quoting higher prices. Subsequent owners who engage the architect will pay more for their projects than they would for the same work by another architect known to be fair. Eventually "advocate" architects lose work from savvy owners because the owners know it will cost more. Therefore, administering the owner/contractor agreement one-sidedly is bad for the architect's practice. Architects sometimes must refuse owners an unreasonable request, but most disputes an architect has to deal with during construction are in the opposite direction: getting the contractor to execute the work as per plans and specifications, to the quality for which the owner has contracted and is entitled, on the agreed schedule.

The timing for the schematic design, design development, and construction document phases is set by a schedule mutually agreed upon by the owner and the architect. Once construction begins, however, the schedule is mainly in the hands of the contractor. For this reason, architects define in the owner/architect agreement the duration of their obligation to provide contract administration services.

Normally the construction administration phase begins at the time the owner/contractor agreement is signed, or "executed" (an ominous-sounding term). At this signing (sometimes accompanied by a celebration including champagne), the owner and the contractor each sign three complete sets of **contract documents**, including the working drawings, the project manual, bid addenda, and the contract itself, plus any amendments or riders. Typically the owner, the con-

tractor, and the architect each keep one signed set. These are official legal documents; they should not be marked up or used for general daily reference.

The architect's standard services in the construction administration phase normally end at either **final completion** (when all the contractor's obligations to the owner, other than the guarantee period, have been met) or sixty days after **substantial completion** (when the premises are able to be occupied for their intended use, but short of the completion of the "punchlist," or list of minor incomplete items), whichever is earlier. Someone once said the first 90 percent of a job takes 90 percent of the time, and the last 10 percent takes the other 90 percent of the time. An architect could end up spending a lot of time (and money) chasing after contractors for months (or years) getting them to complete the last items and would be very unhappy to have to foot the bill for another party's failure to complete. If time beyond the sixty days after substantial completion is required, it should be considered a **change in service** (discussed on page 72), and the architect should bill the owner for additional compensation. If the delay is caused by a contractor, the contractor should reimburse the owner for these additional fees.

As discussed at the beginning of this chapter, the architect has the general obligations to act as the owner's representative (to the extent agreed upon with the owner), to keep the owner informed of the progress and status of the project, to make decisions that are consistent with the intent of the contract documents, and to secure performance by both the owner and the contractor that conforms to the contract documents. It is just as important to be sure the owner pays the contractor by the deadlines set in the agreement as it is to see that the contractor uses, say, the exact wood listed in the specifications.

Architects must make periodic *site observations* at intervals they, in their sole professional judgment, feel are necessary to fulfill their obligations. Avoid promising a visit every *x* days or *y* times a week: at some points in a project it might be appropriate to be on site every day; at other times once a week is adequate. You are there to see that the work generally is progressing according to schedule and generally is being done according to the scope and quality required in the contract documents. While you must try to protect the owner against defects and shortcomings in the work, you are *not* required to make detailed, exhaustive inspections or be on-site continuously. The architect's level of observation is often the subject of debate (and lawsuits). A full-time on site representative from the architect's office, sometimes known as a "clerk of the works," can be provided (at an additional cost) to the owner. While architects do their best, within reason, to protect the owner, it is ultimately the contractor's responsibility and obligation to do the job as per the contract documents. The

architect has the right vis-à-vis the contractor and the obligation to the owner to reject any work that does not conform to the documents. If at all in doubt, the architect should discuss specific instances of observed nonconformance with the owner. If, in the architect's professional judgment, such issues of nonconformance to the contract documents do not affect public health and safety, the owner may elect, as a business decision, to accept them, perhaps with a reduction in the contract sum. The architect should not make such decisions without consulting the owner.

Architects do make *inspections*, usually at the time of substantial completion and at final completion, to certify to the owner that the contractor has, to the best of the architect's judgment and belief (which means it is a judgment, not a guarantee), completed the work per the contract documents to have achieved substantial or final completion. Inspections are more thorough and intense than observations.

Clients sometimes ask if you will "supervise the construction work." While architects indeed endeavor to protect the owner's interests during construction, as described above, they don't actually "supervise" in a formal sense. The word has specific legal meanings. The construction workers are not in the architect's employ—they work for the contractor—so the architect *can't* supervise them. "Supervision" carries a responsibility, under many states' laws, that architects can't satisfy and aren't insured for—for example, providing workers' compensation insurance coverage. Architects do, of course, supervise their own employees.

Architects draw and specify the final result to be built; only in unusual circumstances is the actual process of achieving it described in the plans and specs, and then typically for an exotic or uncommon component. The process is generically called **construction means and methods**, and it is a contractor's responsibility. For example, the architect may draw an interior partition of light-gauge metal studs, clad in gypsum drywall, taped, spackled, and painted. If the contractor has a way of putting up the gypsum drywall first and slipping in the studs last that achieves the exact partition drawn, that should be okay with the architect, because the end result is as specified. The order of work is the contractor's construction-means-and-methods business. The architect may specify that the ceiling shall be painted but doesn't instruct the contractor to tell the painter to use a ladder or a Baker scaffold to get to it. If the painter hires birds with paint brushes and the ceiling is painted per spec, it's fine with me. (The union may object, but that's the contractor's business.)

Safety on the job site is also the contractor's responsibility. The contractor should have a safety plan that conforms to OSHA (see chapter 2) and all local regulations and an enforcement program to ensure conformance to that plan. Still, if you see something happening on a job site that looks dangerous, say so. Notify the contractor or, if he or she is not present, the site superintendent. If the problem is not remedied, notify the owner. If it still is not corrected, you may have to notify the appropriate regulatory authorities, such as the Building Department or Building Inspector.

An architect in our office was once leading an elderly inspecting engineer through a site, taking him to the back of the building, a brownstone being renovated, so he could inspect work on the rear masonry wall. She walked around the opening in the floor that had been made for a new elevator shaft and was covered by a sheet of gypsum drywall. When the engineer, following behind her, walked across it, he crashed and fell down two stories. Our architect ran down the two flights to help the engineer, called 911, notified his wife, went with him in the ambulance to the hospital, and waited for his wife to arrive. The engineer was very shaken but luckily suffered only a broken rib. Our architect may not have done what she was contractually *required* to do—safety on the site is the contractor's job—but doing the right *human* thing is always the best thing to do. The outcome: the contractor, the subcontractors, everyone on the job was sued; we were not, possibly because we had a thoughtful and caring architect on the project.

In order to provide order, clarity, and consistency of instructions on a project, it is essential that there be a chain of command and a **communication protocol** that is clearly stated in both the standard owner/architect agreement and the owner/contractor agreement, so all parties (and their subparties) have mutually consented to the standards. The owner needs one spokesperson through whom all the owner's constituents speak and who has authority to act for the owner. The owner should communicate with the contractor through the architect; communication with the subcontractors is properly through the contractor, and with the consultants through the architect. Not adhering to the protocol causes confusion, miscommunication, finger-pointing, and misconceptions about proper responsibility. When a contractor goes directly to an owner and proposes a better way of doing something, the owner should tell the contractor to submit it to the architect for consideration. It may indeed be a "better way"; it may also be a less expensive way that will not perform as necessary. The architect is better qualified than the owner to make the judgment.

All communications between the parties should be in writing—people often have self-serving memories about what was said. Moreover, issues are sometimes resolved many months (and even years) after the communications occurred, when even the best of memories may be hazy, and certainly impossible to prove. A good rule of thumb: if it wasn't written, it didn't happen.

Processing submittals from the contractor is an important function of the architect during construction. Submittals called for in the project manual are sent during the course of the work to the architect, who reviews them for conformance to the design intent and points out nonconformance to specification requirements. Missing nonconformance does not relieve the contractor of the obligation to meet the specs fully. It is not the architect's responsibility to check the accuracy of the field dimensions shown on shop drawings, which are measured on site by the subcontractor preparing the "shops," but the architect should call out anything that appears egregiously incorrect. Keep a *submittal log* (see fig. 5.1) that shows what submittals are required, when they were submitted, whether you sent them on to relevant consultants, when you returned them to the contractor, and what action should be taken by the contractor or subcontractor (for example, "ok," "ok as noted," "ok to proceed but resubmit for record purposes," "resubmit for further review prior to proceeding"). Carefully and accurately document the flow of the submittals, and act on them thoroughly and promptly. Some contractors insist on deadlines for the architect's actions (*x* days from submission, or the submittal will be considered approved or will be a legitimate cause for a delay claim by the contractor). This may be a realistic defense against architects who don't act in a timely fashion, but it is also a potential liability for the architect. Our firm usually accepts deadlines if the submittals are presented in an orderly fashion according to an agreed-upon schedule. This prevents a contractor from saving up submittals, delivering a

SHOP DRAWING SUBMISSIONS LOG   October 1, 2006

PROJECT:
Additions to
New City School
700 East 75th Street
New York, NY
#0236

STATUS LEGEND:
A = Approved
AAN = Approved as noted
R = Rejected/Revise and Resubmit
AAN/RR = Approved as Noted/Revise and Resubmit
AAN/RFR = Approved as Noted/Resubmit for Record

Number	Description	Name of Subcontractor	Received from GC	Sent to Consultant	Name of Consultant	Received from Consultant	Returned to Contractor	Status
06400-1	Millwork at Pantry	Astoria Cabinetry	08.25.06				08.31.06	AAN
09650-1	Rubber Base	Master Flooring	08.13.06				08.17.06	AAN
09650-2	VCT	Master Flooring	08.13.06				08.19.06	AAN
09680-1	Carpet	Master Flooring	08.13.06				08.19.06	AAN
09900-1	Paint	Walls, Inc.	08.22.06				08.28.06	AAN/RR
10100-1	Blinds	Windows & Shades, Co.	08.13.06				08.19.06	AAN
10100-2	Radiator Enclosure	Astoria Cabinetry	08.19.06				08.25.06	AAN
15000-1	Trane Unit	Lawrence Mech	08.11.06	08.11.06	KRM	08.13.06	08.15.06	AAN
15000-2	Sheet metal dwg	Lawrence Mech	08.12.06	08.12.06	KRM	08.12.06	08.14.06	R
15000-3	Air Outlet Submittal	Lawrence Mech			KRM	08.18.06	08.20.06	R
15000-3-2	Air Outlet Submittal	Lawrence Mech			KRM	08.27.06	08.30.06	AAN
15000-4	Vibration Isolators	Lawrence Mech	08.21.06	08.21.06	KRM	08.25.06	08.27.06	AAN
15300-1	Sink and Faucet Cuts	DTR	08.17.06				08.21.06	AAN
16500-1	Light Fixtures	DTR	08.12.06	08.13.06	KRM	08.13.06	08.16.06	AAN/RR

5.1 Submittal Log

truckload at one time, and overwhelming the architect's project team for the purpose of making a delay claim. A pre-approved schedule for review of submittals is fair to both the contractor and the architect.

During any construction project there will be questions, some caused by lack of clarity of the documents, some by unforeseen conditions. Contractors should submit all questions in writing in the form of a **Request for Information** (RFI) and the architect should answer in writing, usually within an agreed-upon and prompt time—for example, a week. If the answer involves a potential change (whether caused by the owner, the architect, or the contractor), the architect prepares a **Notice of Proposed Change** (NPC), fully describing the change. (Don't you love all these abbreviations?) The contractor reviews the NPC, and determines whether it will cause a change (up or down) of the contract sum and whether it will increase or decrease the construction period. This information is then presented to the architect as a **Proposed Change Order** (PCO); the architect reviews it and discusses it with the owner. If acceptable, it is made into a **Change Order** (CO), which accurately describes the change in scope of work, contract sum, and contract period. The change order is signed by the contractor, the architect, and the owner, and then it becomes an integral part of the contract documents.

Periodically (usually monthly) as per the owner/contractor agreement, the contractor prepares a **Requisition for Payment** (req) consisting of a *requisition certificate* and a *continuation sheet*. The former spells out the original contract sum, changes that have been made and agreed to, and the current contract sum. It summarizes the work to date (as detailed in the continuation sheet), payments to date, and amount currently due. If the architect agrees with the information presented, he or she approves it and signs the certificate. The architect should make a site visit at the final date covered by the requisition to evaluate information in the continuation sheet, which lists every trade of work, the full value of that trade, the portion of the work completed to the date of the requisition, and the calculated amount thus due (the full amount times the percentage complete), from which is subtracted the *retainage*, usually a fixed percentage of the amount due (described in greater detail in chapter 8, under "Payments and Completion"). These values are totaled and become the amounts shown on the certificate, which is the face sheet of the requisition. Most contractors now use electronic versions of the AIA G701 Certificate and the G702 Continuation Sheet, or schedule. The architect's job in processing requisitions is to evaluate the status of each trade on the job and see that the amount done in the field is the same amount shown on the req, to document any differences, to correct the req (if necessary) or have the contractor make the corrections and resubmit the req, and to forward it to the owner within seven days of receipt. Architects must take care not to approve

amounts greater than are actually in place, because if the contractor defaults (or even disappears), the architect could be held responsible for the amount "over-req'd." Like submittals, requisitions must be attended to promptly by the architect.

I was once an expert witness for an architect being sued by an owner, whose contractor had been convicted of mail fraud and sent to prison, and so (obviously) did not finish the project. The owner claimed that because the architect had over-req'd, the contractor was paid more money than there was work on the job; completing the project with another contractor would therefore cost more than agreed to. And the architect should pay the difference, which was a lot. (The case was settled, and the architect did pay.)

At the contractor's request, the architect makes inspections for substantial and final completion; when the architect is satisfied they have been accomplished, the architect prepares certificates attesting to it. At substantial completion, the architect prepares the *punchlist*, a list of all items of uncompleted or incorrectly done work, gives it to the owner to review (and make reasonable additions), and submits it to the contractor. At final completion, the architect checks to see that all items on the punchlist have been completed or corrected, that the contractor has submitted all *close-out documents*, such as guarantees, warranties, final waivers of liens (sworn statements that no claims will be made against the project for nonpayment) from contractors, subcontractors, material suppliers, and other suppliers, and anything else required in the contract documents.

And the job is done!

Changes in Services

That is, the job is done if the architect is providing the classic, normal standard services. Other services, which architects are qualified to do, can be provided for additional compensation. Although the list of changes in service is almost infinite, some of the most common ones are listed here:

- preparing the program for the project
- assisting the owner in site selection
- providing a clerk of the works
- evaluating an excessive number of change orders
- changing previously approved drawings
- changing the documents due to a substantive change in the project size, quality, complexity, schedule, or budget
- assisting in correction of fire or water damage or vandalism
- assisting in litigation (to which the architect is not a party)
- providing services to complete the project after sixty days beyond substantial completion

- carrying out post-occupancy evaluations
- doing the project as multiple prime contracts or as "fast track"
- providing assistance in corrective work or retrofitting
- providing inspections prior to end of guarantee periods

Including the list of some of the potential changes in scope of services in an agreement is useful because it helps clarify that those services are not part of the standard services package for the standard services fee.

To summarize, the professional services architects perform for owners include: the general services provided in every phase; the five normal phases provided as standard services in most arrangements, and some other services that architects can provide in addition to the standard services. The difference between standard services and changes in service is important because it affects fees (the subject of the next chapter), which also explains the importance of clearly defining precisely what services are to be provided for the specific project under consideration.

6 Fees for Architects' Services

Fee Bases

Traditional fee arrangements are based on a percentage of construction cost, fixed fee, or time charges, and sometimes a combination of these. It is important to understand the "big three"—the pros and cons and suitability of each in particular situations. Alternative arrangements are discussed later in the section "Other Methods of Compensation."

The most important consideration in choosing a fee structure is that its flexibility match that of the services to be provided. An architect's office can't be Bob's Big Boy Restaurant: all you can eat for $6.95. A *limited fee* must be for limited services in the interests of fairness (as well as avoiding bankruptcy). If the scope of services to be provided is proposed (or expected) to be open-ended, so must be the fee.

As described in chapter 5, the services that an architect provides to an owner typically are of two kinds. First are services required in the normal course of projects, called *standard services*: schematic design, design development, construction documents, bidding and negotiation, and construction administration phases. The second set of services is *changes in scope of services*; these include services that many architects are qualified and experienced to offer but are not generally required to provide. An owner may elect to have the architect add these services to the list of things to be done, and the fee would naturally be higher than if the architect were providing only standard services.

Sometimes you don't know before starting a project exactly what services will be needed, but as the project develops the scope of services broadens and you must charge an additional fee for them. Such changes might include the cost of redesign if an owner changes the requirements of a project after the architect creates designs for the original program, or if additional work is needed as a result of a fire during construction or a failed contractor.

Fees for Standard Services

In order to choose the right method of charging for standard services and determining what the fees for them should be, you need to understand how the three most common methods work. The terms and conditions described here are typical, but like everything else in practice, they may be modified to suit the specific situation and the nature of the actual parties. Determining the right fee is complex. How special are the services you are providing (as opposed to a "commodity," something that any firm could offer)? What kind of client is it, and how sensitive is it to cost (and how important to the client is a high level of expertise and service)? How experienced are you in negotiating fees: Can you assess the cost to the firm to provide the services needed? What would the competition charge? Are the services offered unique and therefore worth more to the owner?

Whichever fee method is selected, the owner should pay the architect an initial payment before any services are rendered, upon signature of the owner/architect agreement; it will be credited to the owner at the time of the final payment. The initial payment is usually between one and two months of the architect's expected billing.

Percentage-of-construction-cost Basis

The classic method of compensation for architects' services is the *percentage-of-construction-cost* basis. (See fig. 6.1, a sample billing on a project with a percentage-of-construction-cost fee of 11 percent.) As the name implies, the fee is computed by multiplying the construction cost by an agreed-upon percentage. The percentage is related to the size and complexity of the project. A warehouse takes less time to design and build per construction dollar spent than a hospital, so the percentage would reasonably be lower; a large project such as a $40 million apartment house takes less time per construction dollar than does a $40,000 house addition, so it would command a lower percentage.

"Lower" and "higher" are pretty vague. What is the range of these percentages? An experienced architect knows from past projects what costs will be reasonable, and by relating them to relevant known

---

CAMERON   DAVIS   ARCHITECTS   LLP
123 BROADWAY SUITE 5005 NEW YORK NY 10006 (212) 675-4355

Avery Washington
Business Manager
New City School
700 East 75th Street
New York, NY 10128

PROJECT:
Additions to
New City School
700 East 75th Street
New York, NY
#0236

STATEMENT: Professional Services: August 1 through August 31:

Fee for Standard Services
Based on 11% fee and $2,300,000 Construction Cost
Fee = $253,000.00

Phase of Work	Percentage of Total Fee for Phase	Fee for Phase	Portion of Phase Completed to Date	Fee Due for Phase to Date
Schematic Design	15%	$37,950.00	80%	$30,360.00
Design Development	20%	$50,600.00	20%	$10,120.00
Construction Document	40%	$101,200.00	5%	$5,060.00
Bidding & Negotiations	5%	$12,650.00	0%	$0.00
Construction Admin	20%	$50,600.00	0%	$0.00
Total	100%	$253,000.00		$45,540.00
Paid to date (not including intial payment, to be credited to final statement):				$6,100.00

Total Due this Statement for Standard Services: $39,440.00

Payment Due by September 15, 2006

August 31, 2006

6.1 Sample statement for professional services, or invoice, on a project with a percentage-of-construction-cost fee. It shows the percentage, the construction cost, and the resultant fee; and it breaks down the fee per phase of work, the portion of each phase completed to date, and the fee due at the time of the statement, after giving credit for payments to date.

building costs he or she can derive a fair percentage. Until the mid-1970s, if you were not familiar with the exact type or scope of a project for which you were preparing a fee proposal, you could check the AIA's Minimum Fee Schedule, which set out percentages based on the size and complexity of a given project. But the U.S. Department of Justice decided that if architects who should be competitors (members of the AIA) were setting minimum fees for their services, they were violating the Sherman Antitrust Act, which was designed to prevent collusion to fix prices. The AIA therefore withdrew the fee schedules and ceased recommending any fees, minimum or otherwise, to its members. Notwithstanding, today you can find virtually identical fee schedules published in construction-cost data books published by both F. W. Dodge and R. S. Means, two industry publishing companies, and other sources. These schedules are described as "the necessary fees for good professional services," or "those fees below which adequate services should not be expected." They are permitted because those publishing them are independent sources reporting on practice, not professionals agreeing on what they themselves should be paid.

I have discussed the "percentage" part of the arrangement. What is the "construction cost"? This question is not as dumb as it sounds. For a completed project, the construction cost is the full amount paid to the contractor, including changes and extras. It does not include architects' and engineers' professional fees, the cost of land, or the cost of any money borrowed to pay for the construction. These added to the construction cost make up the overall *project cost*.

What if the work is never built? Sometimes owners abandon a project before beginning construction but after the architect has done a lot of design work, perhaps even prepared construction documents. Is the "construction cost" (and thus the architect's fee) zero? No. Such a fee arrangement would make architects' work highly speculative, resembling the way real estate brokers typically charge: no fee unless the transaction is completed. Even if a project is not built, the architect gets paid for the portion of the services provided. Usually, 80 percent of the architect's fee is earned by the time the "shovel breaks ground" and construction starts. So, what is the "construction cost" for a project where no money ever is paid to a contractor? It is the latest, best estimate of what the cost would have been had the project proceeded. Before bidding takes place, that would be an early estimate or the architect's "statement of probable cost"; after bidding, the construction cost for fee-computation purposes is the lowest bona fide bid. Say a project is terminated after it has been bid, but before any construction work begins. In most agreements, the architect performed 80 percent of his or her services by that time. If the agreed-upon fee was set at 15 percent of the construction cost, and the low bid was $2,000,000, the architect would be due 80 percent of the 15 percent fee of the $2,000,000 construction cost—80 percent x 15 percent x $2,000,000—or $240,000, not including any separate additional termination costs. Every architect at some point has a client who abandons a project and genuinely (but mistakenly) believes the architect's work should be free. Fortunately, all good standard contracts make that impermissible.

If a client really wants you to work on spec, you could reasonably do that if, before work began, you set your fees high enough to cover the cost of work done for unbuilt projects. Then the clients who go ahead with their projects in effect pay for those who don't. This seems to me like a bad idea.

The advantage of the percentage-of-construction-cost fee is that it automatically adjusts the fee for changes in the size of a project, its location, and related construction-cost differences (the costs of doing business may vary from one region to another, in terms of salaries, rents, and so on), and level of construction quality. The major disadvantage of the percentage-of-construction-cost fee is that it looks like a conflict of interest for the architect, who benefits when the owner has to spend more money on the contractor. But in fact architects try to use owners' construction money wisely and efficiently and protect owners from excessive charges.

Fixed-fee Basis

The second type of fee arrangement is a *fixed*, or *set*, *fee*: the architect charges an agreed-upon amount for a defined amount of service. Again, defining the services is the element critical to making this a fair arrangement. Most commonly the fixed fee covers an entire project (see fig. 6.2), but it can also be set for a given unit of a project, say x per room for a hotel, or y per apartment for an apartment house, or z per square foot for the design of a tenant space in a commercial office building (see fig. 6.3). Unit-cost fixed fees work best with experienced owners and architects who are very familiar with the given type of work. The advantage of this fee basis is that it is highly predictable for both parties; the disadvantage is its low level of flexibility. While there would normally still be additional charges for any changes in scope of services beyond what is clearly defined in the agreement, the architect must be very disciplined to perform profitably. For certain types of work, such as projects with parts that are repetitive in nature, and with knowledgeable owners, it is certainly the most common way of providing services.

Time-charge Basis

The third common method of compensation for architects' services is the *time charge*: the architect charges the client on an hourly basis

STATEMENT

October 31, 2006

Chris Jones
Asst. Dean for Administration
Maxwell Law School
300 Hollywood Blvd.
Los Angeles, CA 90028

PROJECT:

Maxwell Law School
Alterations to Floors 6-10
#0501

Statement for Professional Services:
October 1, 2006 through October 31, 2006

Fees for Professional Services
Standard Services, based on fixed fee of $650,000

Phase of Work	Fee for Phase as per Agreement	Portion of Phase Completed to Date	Fee Due for Phase	Fee Invoiced to Date	Fee Due this Statement
Schematic Design	$65,000	100%	$65,000	$65,000	$0.00
Design Development	$115,000	95%	$109,250	$92,500	$16,750.00
Construction Documents	$230,000	50%	$115,000	$21,250	$93,750.00
Bidding & Negotiations	$35,000	5%	$1,750	$0	$1,750.00
Construction Admin	$205,000	0%	$0	$0	$0.00
Total Standard Services: $650,000		44.77%	$291,000	$178,750	$112,250.00

Total Due this Statement: $112,250.00

Payment Due by November 15, 2006

**785 Wilshire Blvd. 16th Fl
Los Angeles, CA 90017
213.546.5555**
www.wilsonmoorearchitects.com

6.2 Sample statement for professional services on a project with a fixed fee for standard services.

THOMSON - HARRIS - YOUNG
ARCHITECTS

Pat Taylor
CFO
Investments, Inc.
945 Wabash Ave Suite 420
Chicago, IL 60605

PROJECT:
New Offices for Investments, Inc.
321W Washington Street
Chicago, IL
#0428

STATEMENT: For Period: March 1, 2006 through March 31, 2006

Fee for Professional Services
Based on 60,000 rentable square feet at $3.50 per rentable square foot= $210,000 fee for Standard Services

PHASE OF WORK	PERCENTAGE OF TOTAL FEE FOR PHASE	PORTION OF PHASE COMPLETED TO DATE	PERCENT OF FEE DUE TO DATE	FEE DUE TO DATE
Schematic Design	15%	95%	14.25%	$29,925.00
Design Development	20%	70%	14%	$29,400.00
Consruction Documents	40%	15%	6%	$1,260.00
Bidding & Negotiations	5%	0%	0%	$0.00
Construction Admin	20%	0%	0%	$0.00
TOTAL	100%		34.25%	$60,585.00
Paid to date, not including initial payment (which will be credited to final statement)				$16,585.00
Due This Period for Fee for Standard Services				$44,000.00

Total Due: $44,000.00

Payment Due by April 15, 2006

March 31, 2006

644 N MICHIGAN AVE CHICAGO IL 60611 TEL: 999 6568

6.3 Sample statement for professional services where the fee is determined on a set unit-cost basis—in this case, $3.50 per rentable square foot.

for the time actually spent on the project. Rates are agreed upon in advance and usually vary according to the level of personnel working on the project: senior staff are billed at higher rates than less experienced staff. The rates are established in one of two ways. The first way, like billing by other professionals such as lawyers and accountants, is simply to set rates for each level of the staff. For example, partners or principals are billed at a per hour, senior architects at b per hour, architects at c per hour, and junior designers at d per hour. The list is part of the agreement and customarily includes notice that hourly rates may be adjusted annually during the course of the project. Most architects feel this is the easy way to explain terms to and bill the average client. Figure 6.4 is a sample statement based on this method.

The second way of setting hourly rates for design professionals historically has been the "multiple" method used with experienced clients such as governments, large corporations, or institutions that have substantial ongoing building programs and regularly procure professional design services. To achieve the billing rate for staff members (as opposed to owners of the architect firms, who are called either "principals" or "partners," depending on the legal structure of the firm—see chapter 10), multiply the staffer's salary by a computed factor that adds the cost of "mandatory and customary benefits." "Mandatory" benefits are the pro-rata share of the employee's

government-required expense such as the employer's share of Federal Insurance Contributions Act (FICA; the employee's share is deducted and sent to the government at each pay period); unemployment insurance; and workers' compensation insurance. "Customary" benefits may include the employer's cost of vacation, sick, and holiday time, health insurance, retirement plans, and any other benefits that the employer gives its employees. Mandatory and customary costs add to the actual cost of employees for every hour the employees work on clients' projects. The actual amount varies from firm to firm, but benefits normally add 25 to 40 percent to the actual salary cost. The full hourly rate of salary plus cost of benefits is called the Direct Personnel Expense (DPE). We're not done yet. On top of DPE, a firm must add in overhead (OH), other actual costs of doing business besides the direct costs of the people doing direct client work, as described in the DPE. Overhead includes office rent, telephones, furniture, computers, software, copiers, scanners, printers, plotters, and other equipment, as well as support-staff time (secretaries and administrative assistants, who are necessary to make a firm work but don't do direct project work). Finally, in addition to the DPE and the OH (which is usually about equal to the DPE), the hourly billing rate should include the firm's profit, which is determined by the firm's goals as well as the marketplace. Figure 6.5 is a sample statement based on this method.

MOUNTAIN
D E S I G N
ARCHITECTS

110 BLAKE STREET SUITE 300 DENVER CO 80202 T: 303 123 9876 F: 303 123 9870

Kim Robertson
President
Robertson, Inc.
244 Madison Street
Denver, CO 80206

PROJECT:
New Offices for Robertson, Inc.
100 Park Street
Denver, CO
#7924532

STATEMENT: Professional Services: February 1, 2006 through February 28, 2006

Fees for Professional Services

Standard Services, based on agreed-upon rates:

	Hrs	Rate	Fee
Partners:			
Bruce Johnson, FAIA	6	$200/hr	$1,200.00
Dale Jones, AIA	4	$200/hr	$800.00
Senior Architects:			
Lisa Cunningham, AIA	18	$120/hr	$2,160.00
David Goldberger, AIA	10	$120/hr	$1,200.00
Designers:			
Consuela Costas	20	$95/hr	$1,900.00
Total Standard Services:	**58**		**$7,260.00**

| **Total Due this Statement:** | | | **$7,260.00** |

Payment Due by March 15, 2006

February 28, 2006

Alen + Hall Architects
700 Alaskan Way South
Seattle WA 98104

TO	PROJECT
Robin Clark	Expressway Overpass
Director of Highways	Improvements
King County Highway Dept.	#0515
Seattle, WA	

STATEMENT

For Professional Services: June 1, 2006 through June 30, 2006:

FEES FOR PROFESSIONAL SERVICES

Standard Services:

	Salary/Hr	Hrs	Fee
Dianne Robertson	$38/hr	17	$646.00
Chris McPearson	$32/hr	25	$800.00
Richard Baldisconi	$21/hr	98	$2,058.00
Total Salaries:			$3,504.00
Total Direct Personnel Expense (Salary + 32%)=			$4,625.28
With Overhead & Profit (DPE + 135%)=			$10,869.41

Total Due this Statement: **$10,869.41**

Payment Due by July 15, 2006

June 30, 2006

6.4 Sample statement for professional services under an agreement where the architect is charging for time at agreed-upon (set) rates, without a maximum for those charges.

6.5 Sample statement for professional services based on a "multiple" system.

The sum of all these components becomes the final multiple of the DPE, producing the actual rate per employee billed to the client. Typically, the final billing rate might be between 2.0 and 3.0 times the DPE. For example:

Salary for Jane Doe:	$20/hour (about $42,000/year)
Benefits rate for firm:	35%
Benefits/hour for Jane Doe:	35% x $20/hr = $7.00/hr
DPE for Jane Doe:	$27/hour
Firm's overhead:	110% of DPE
OH for Jane Doe:	110% x $27/hr = $29.70/hr
DPE + OH for Jane Doe:	$27 + $29.70 = $56.70
Profit for firm:	15% of DPE + OH
Profit for Jane Doe:	15% x $56.70 = $8.50/hour
Billing rate for Jane Doe:	$56.70/hr + $8.50/hr = $65.20/hr

If you find the multiple method of billing as difficult to understand as I do to explain it, you can see why this is a tough method for inexperienced clients to understand and why many architects don't use it unless required to do so by the client. The clients' eyes glaze over; they clearly think you are a lunatic. In our early practice, the few who did make an effort to understand asked questions I couldn't (or didn't want to) answer: Why did we give that amount of vacation? Should Le Corbusier's birthday really be a paid holiday? How did we arrive at that level of profit? So whenever possible, we bill like the rest of the world: so much per hour for Sally, and so much per hour for Jim. Nevertheless, you do have to understand multiples for those huge clients with their world-changing projects.

When you bill on a time-charge basis, is there a cap, a ceiling, or a maximum that the charges can amount to, or is your compensation open-ended? As with percentage-of-construction-cost and fixed-fee methods, a cap must be related to a scope of services that is clearly defined in the agreement. Even with a clear limitation on scope, which reduces the architect's exposure to losing money by having to provide more services than expected, there is no upside of making a greater profit if the work can be done very efficiently, as is the case with the percentage-of-construction-cost and fixed-fee methods. The time-charge-with-a-cap method is a "heads you win, tails I lose" proposition: the architect is penalized for things not going smoothly, but not rewarded if they do.

Time charges without a cap, or open-ended time charges, is in many ways the fairest arrangement for the architect. Neither architect nor client is taking a huge gamble; neither stands to have a major win or loss. Although many other professionals are compensated this way, many clients find it uncomfortable because it lacks predictability and the fees can mount up considerably—good architecture takes more time than inexperienced clients expect. One advantage of the arrangement is that besides reducing the architect's risk, it forces clients to better value and respect the architect's time.

The open-ended time charge is the only method of billing that does not require a defined scope of services, and for that reason it is often the most appropriate for the beginning stages of a project, when the scope is still being explored, or for projects in which the unanticipated is expected.

It should be obvious that no one billing method is best for all projects or all stages of a given project. For more exploratory and unique projects, those that have more unusual programs or expectations, the open-ended time charge is the more flexible format and may be more appropriate. Furthermore, while some phases of an architect's work, such as construction documents, can be well controlled by the architect, and reasonably done for a predetermined fee, for other phases time charges may be a preferable method to deal with unforeseeable circumstances during design and construction administration. For example, the low bidder may have become the low bidder by providing less administrative (or competent) staff to execute the project smoothly, thereby causing more work for the architect at a lower fee, if on the percent-of-construction-cost basis.

Some of an architect's work is pretty routine, while some requires inspiration and high levels of creativity. Should all these hours be charged at the same rate? If all jobs, architects, and owners were the same, there would probably only be one, perfectly evolved fee method. Since they are all different (not to mention that the world isn't perfect), there are many alternatives and combinations. The three basic methods are a good place to start to fashion an appropriate fee arrangement, one that provides the services on behalf of the owner to wisely utilize, conserve, and protect the owner's resources of money, time, energy, and land, and to compensate the architect fairly for his or her skill, experience, efforts, and risk. Very often, spending a little more for the architect's fee saves the client a lot more on other costs.

Other Methods of Compensation

The three methods of payment outlined above are the norms, but some alternatives deserve consideration. They provide a smaller up-front payment for the architect in exchange for a share of the owner's profits later on. One arrangement calls for the architect to receive a portion (or all the fee) by taking an equity position, or share of ownership, in a project. In a large project such as a rental commercial space, the architect could earn a long-term stream of income from a share of the rental profits, rather than a one-time fee. On a residential, owner-user project such as a custom house, the architect's limited share of ownership could generate a payment the first (or every) time the property is sold. The architect's share might be a percentage of either the capital gain (the increase in value of the property, or the sale price less the cost of the land and the house) or the sale price on each sale. Another arrangement, similar to a musician's or author's royalty, calls for the architect to be paid on an ongoing basis for the use of the building.

These alternatives raise some potentially thorny conflict-of-interest issues. For instance, during construction the architect is expected to be even-handed between the owner and the contractor in administering the agreement; when the architect is in effect a part-owner, impartiality could be compromised. With due consideration, openness, and transparency, these conflicts can be resolved.

Change in Scope of Services

As previously noted, whenever a fee is not open-ended, it must be tied to a clearly defined scope of services that the architect is to provide for that fee. If the need arises for the architect to provide other services, this change in scope of services is described in the owner/architect agreement together with the method of charging for the services. The usual method is the time-charge (see fig. 6.6), but

another arrangement can be specified when the services are needed. Many agreements require the owner's written agreement for additional charges *before* the architect provides them; some simply require the architect to notify the owner that such services are needed, and the owner will be required to pay for them unless the owner promptly objects in writing. What these various contractual provisions have in common is ***prior notification***. Failing to notify the owner makes fees for additional services harder to collect. Fair warning: if, before providing certain changes in scope of services, you don't tell the owner that these services are not part of the package of standard services, be prepared to have a hard time collecting.

If you are working on a time-charge basis without a cap, the issue of standard services versus changes in scope of services never comes up. You perform all services that you deem necessary, and you bill for those services (fig. 6.4 or 6.5).

Reimbursable Expenses

All the fees discussed to this point are for services provided by the architect, the architect's staff, and engineers whom the architect retains as part of the architect's fee for standard services, by agreement, which usually include normal structural and MEPS engineering services. Not included are ***reimbursable expenses***–out-of-pocket

Left Statement

Martinez Architecture & Design

STATEMENT

Blaire Brooke
Director of Operations
Central Hotels, Inc.
1 Center Place
Dallas, TX

Project:
New Hotel
#0519

Professional Services: May 1, 2006 through May 31, 2006:

Fees for Professional Services:

Standard Services: based on an agreed-upon fixed fee of $750,000

Phase of Work	Fee for Phase, as per Agreement	Portion of Phase Completed to Date	Fee Due for Phase to Date	Fee Invoiced to Date	Fee Due this Statement
Schematic Design	$90,000	100%	$90,000	$90,000	$0.00
Design Development	$110,000	90%	$99,000	$92,500	$6,500.00
Consruction Documents	$275,000	40%	$110,000	$21,250	$88,750.00
Bidding & Negotiations	$30,000	10%	$3,000	$0	$3,000.00
Construction Admin	$245,000	0%	$0	$0	$0.00
Total Standard Services	$750,000	40.93%	$307,000	$203,750	$98,250.00

Change of Scope of Serveces this period: on a time-charge basis:
Change in design of Reception Area

Partners
Dakota Martinez, FAIA — 3.00 hrs @ $200.00/hr — $600.00
Senior Designers
Courtney Smith — 18.00 hrs @ $115.00/hr — $2,070.00
Designer
Jane Cox — 9.00 hrs @ $95.00/hr — $855.00

Total Additional Services: $3,525.00

Reimbursable Expenses this Period (see attached bills):

Reproductions / delivery	$1,413.00
Department of Buildings Consultant	$2,000.00
Total Reimbursable Expenses:	$3,413.00

Total Due this Statement: $105,188.00
Payment Due by June 15, 2006
May 31, 2006

323 Ross Avenue Dallas TX 75202 (214) 444 5566 (214) 444 5577

Right Statement

STATEMENT

For Period November 1, 2006 through November 30, 2006

LEE MILLER ARCHITECTURE
1771 S Central Ave
Phoenix AZ 85004
602.345.3344
www.lma.pro

TO	PROJECT	DATE
Drew Jones, CFO	New Offices	November 30, 2006
Cactus Flower Insurance Co.	C.F.I.	
1 W Van Buren St	#0605	
Phoenix, AZ		

FEE FOR PROFESSIONAL SERVICES

PHASE OF WORK	PERCENTAGE OF TOTAL FEE FOR PHASE	PORTION OF PHASE COMPLETED TO DATE	PERCENT OF FEE DUE TO DATE	FEE DUE TO DATE
Schematic Design	15%	95%	14.25%	$24,225.00
Design Development	20%	65%	13%	$22,100.00
Consruction Documents	40%	10%	4%	$6,800.00
Bidding & Negotiations	5%	0%	0%	$0.00
Construction Admin	20%	0%	0%	$0.00
TOTAL	**100%**		**31.25%**	**$53,125.00**
Paid to date, not including initial payment (which will be credited to final statement)				$16,550.00
DUE THIS PERIOD FOR FEE FOR STANDARD SERVICES				**$36,550.00**

REIMBURSABLE EXPENSES

Outside Reprographics:
"Prince of Prints"

11.15.06	Inv: 98907	$428.00	$428.00
11.19.06	Inv: 99112	$219.00	$219.00

The Bindery

11.24.06	Inv: 107302	$52.00	$52.00

In-House Reprographics:

Xeroxes	157 @ $.25/copy =	$39.25
Plotting	273 sf @ $1.75 sf =	$477.75
REIMBURSABLE EXPENSES THIS PERIOD		**$1,216.00**
Administrative Fee, 10%:		$121.60
TOTAL REIMBURSABLE EXPENSES THIS PERIOD		**$1,337.60**

TOTAL DUE, FEE & REIMBURSABLE EXPENSES: $37,887.60

Payment Due by December 15, 2006

6.6 Sample statement for professional services on a project with a fixed fee for standard services. The fee for the change in scope of services is on a time-charge basis. Reimbursable expenses are included in the same statement.

6.7 Sample statement for professional services where the fee is determined on a set unit-cost basis—in this case, $4.00 per rentable square foot. Reimbursable expenses are included in the statement, with a markup, or "administrative fee."

expenses the architect pays to others for items relating to performing professional services. Reimbursable expenses include reproduction costs (large-format copying, plotting, photocopying, and other graphics services), postage and delivery costs, travel and lodging costs in connection with the project, and special consultants (for example, engineers or other consultants beyond the normal engineers' fees described above), as well as preparation of special renderings, promotional or marketing materials, or modelmaking. Some firms charge an additional markup for these items to cover the administrative costs involved (see fig. 6.7).

7 Business Terms of Owner/Architect Agreements

The previous two chapters cover the two main issues of an owner/architect agreement: services and fees. This chapter addresses seven other issues that may be critical: project parameters, instruments of service and copyright law, dispute resolution, consequential damages, publicity and photographic rights, timeliness of payments, and initial payment.

Project Parameters

All the important parameters of a project are listed at the beginning of an agreement:

1. the parties (full legal names, addresses, and authorized representatives of the owner and the architect);

2. the project description, in as much detail as possible (this is protection for the architect and the owner, setting out the scope so that changes in service deserving additional fees or reductions in fees are clear);

3. the budget for the project (again, protection for the owner, if the architect is required to revise the drawings at no additional fee if all the bids come in over an agreed-upon construction budget);

4. the proposed schedule for the project; and

5. the consultants whom the architect is to retain, because this is part of what the owner is "buying."

Instruments of Service and Copyright Law

The sketches, drawings, project manual, and all other work product done by the architect are collectively known as *instruments of service*. In most agreements these are to be produced for an owner for one-time use—building the owner's project—and the architect fully owns all of the work product and the copyrights on it. By paying the agreed-upon fees to the architect, the owner gets the right to the *use* of those documents, but not *ownership* of them. If the owner defaults on the agreement (usually for nonpayment of the fees due), ownership of the documents gives the architect powerful remedies to solve the default. Some owners, though, require the architect to turn over the ownership of documents.

If ownership is not covered, is deleted, or is not mentioned in an agreement, federal copyright law protects architects. It covers both architects' drawings and their actual buildings and prevents them from being copied. Before 1986, copyright just covered drawings, and it was permissible (barring trespassing) for anyone to measure a building, make their own drawings, and build an exact replica. That is not allowed anymore.

Why does it matter? We once designed a house in a small town for an old friend, an attorney. During construction, personal tragedy struck the contractor, who suffered a nervous breakdown and declared bankruptcy, requiring our firm and our client to scramble to find another builder. After the house was completed, a woman telephoned to say that she loved the house and wanted to build an exact copy of it (except that she wanted to reverse the swing on one kitchen cabinet door!). I knew I owned the plans and could sell them to her, but I wanted to discuss the request with the client, who had been involved in the design and valued the fact that his house was unique. I explained to the caller that since her site and probably her needs were different from those of our client, it probably wouldn't be exactly right for her, but I would willingly discuss with her how we might design something right for *her*. We met, but she did not pursue the issue. About a year later our client was very upset to find that his house had been duplicated in a neighboring town by the woman who had called. At that time (there *is* a point to this story) it was legal to copy the building but not the drawings. How did I know she had used our drawings and infringed on the copyright? I looked at her house and found that it matched our plans. But we had made minor adjustments in the field. So, while our client's house didn't match the drawings exactly, hers did! When we checked the Building Department in her town, it was clear that our drawings had been copied, down to the spacing of the drawings on the sheets and certain eccentric labeling. Although we had the proof, my client never went to court: he was busy and so was I, but it was an instructive episode. (It was also interesting to see a building copied with inferior materials and workmanship. Such a "controlled experiment" rarely happens in architecture, and it is vivid proof that the quality does make a difference!)

We were pleased to find that the 1986 copyright law protects architects and their clients even from copying *without* plans.

Dispute Resolution

The relationship between an owner and an architect usually covers a substantial time period and involves some of life's more contentious issues: money, power, and status. It is only natural that there will be some bumps in such a long and winding road. One of the advantages of working with repeat clients, with whom you share values, goals, and respect, is that you are more likely to be able to discuss problems and resolve them to your mutual satisfaction. The solutions may not be perfect for either party but are such that both can live with them. Problems can best be avoided by being open and fair with your client, not hiding problems but dealing with them as quickly as possible (problems are not like fine wine—they rarely improve with age) and doing what you can to reduce their impact. Because there is a tremendous cost, economic, psychic, and career, in not solving problems, it is worth a lot of effort (and sometimes pride and even money) to work them out.

An office building we once built had on the second floor a large rear deck that developed a leak over the occupied first-floor space. We made several suggestions to the client about how to fix it and heard nothing further—until we were sued by the client. Lesson learned: when a client has a problem and you suggest how to fix it, follow up and see if your suggestion solved the problem. If not, work with the client until it *is* solved. This client's idea of a remedy was to remove the deck and rebuild it from scratch, at a projected cost of about $300,000. Because the suit was improperly brought in several ways (explained further in chapter 10), we were able to halt the lawsuit temporarily and discuss the problem with the client and the contractor. It turned out that while some part of the installation may not have been done as per the drawings, the client also had not properly maintained the drains on the deck, which had probably clogged them and contributed to the problem. We were able to persuade the client, the general contractor, and the roofing subcontractor to share equally with us a partial repair, which we believed would solve the problem, costing only $12,000 total, with the understanding that if it didn't work everyone could start suing each other again. Fortunately the simple solution worked well, we paid our $3,000 share, and we solved the problem without major lawsuits—always a preferable outcome.

We have served as expert witnesses in litigations or arbitrations. While not suffering the direct pain of being either plaintiff or defendant in those cases, we have witnessed the cost in time and mental anguish that the parties have put into preparing for the cases, even when they are fully insured.

Sometimes, particularly with the clients you shouldn't have taken on in the first place (as my father says, "you go to bed with dogs, you wake up with fleas"), you can't amicably resolve differences and must solve them some other way. If you don't have a written agreement, or if your owner/architect agreement is silent on how disputes are to be resolved, court is the usual place for settling these matters, either in front of a jury or just before a judge (a bench case).

Many standard owner/architect agreements, though, contemplate other dispute resolution methods. The American Arbitration Association (AAA) has a whole division set up to handle construction disputes. The first step can be ***nonbinding mediation***, in which both parties meet with a mediator, provided by the AAA, and present their sides of the dispute. While both may have their lawyers present, the setting and process is informal, without the strict rules and procedures of a court hearing. After the initial presentations, the mediator often puts the two sides in separate rooms and shuttles back and forth, trying to find common ground and build a compromise solution. A skillful mediator might soften up each side by pointing out the weak points of its arguments and its vulnerabilities. "Nonbinding" means that if both sides don't agree on a solution, either party can bring it to the next level called for in their owner/architect agreement.

The second step can be **binding arbitration**, also arranged by the AAA. Either one arbiter or a panel of three or five arbiters hears both sides of the argument, looks at evidence, and issues a ruling on each of the points in contention. Once the arbiter or arbiters have ruled, neither side can appeal the ruling unless fraud can be proven. Arbitration, like mediation, has the advantage of being informal; its rules are not rigid. It resolves disputes faster and for less cost than does the alternative to mediation and arbitration, which is court. Arbiters are likely to be expert in construction issues and hence better able to deal knowledgably (and less emotionally) than a jury with the complex issues involved. Arbitration is private, an advantage to an unfairly accused professional. (While some people love any kind of publicity, reasonable professionals prefer not to be "tried" in the media.)

Whether disputes are to be resolved in court or by mediation/arbitration, the section on dispute resolution in the owner/architect agreement typically prohibits **joinder**. What this means is that one party (usually the owner) can't sue two other parties together (usually the architect and the contractor) without their permission, which would not very likely be given. Joinder is important, as you'll see in

chapter 10, when I discuss the difference between a **design error** and a **construction error**, and who is responsible for each.

Is it better to resolve disputes in court or by mediation and arbitration? Insurance companies that cover the architect's professional liability, the group that probably has interests most in line with the architect, have no strong preference.

In my view, if you must go to mediation, arbitration, or court, you've already "lost," but sometimes litigation is unavoidable.

Consequential Damages

Consequential damages are indirect losses that result from wrongdoing by one party. For example, an architect designed a roof improperly, so it leaked, damaging a Picasso watercolor that happened to hang directly under the leak. If consequential damages were waived in the owner/architect agreement, the architect is responsible for fixing the leaky roof; if they were not waived, the architect has to fix the leaky roof *and* pay for the Picasso. If an owner's late payment causes an architect to be unable to pay the rent for the office on time, the landlord's late fee would be a consequential damage. You can see that waiving consequential damages is a good idea for both sides and can certainly prevent bogus claims when there are problems.

Publicity and Photographic Rights

In addition to a fee for services, an architect's compensation may include perquisites such as getting wonderful photographs of a job for the portfolio; publication, which can help secure future work; and entry in awards competitions, which may also bring future work. The rights to photography, publicity, and awards should be covered in the owner/architect agreement. Owners should have the right to the privacy of their name, if they wish. So should the architect. ("What?" I can hear you say. Well, if a client has painted a building a vile color or let it deteriorate or made tacky changes to it, do you want your firm credited? If several of your houses are advertised for sale at one time, do you want a potential client to think that nobody wants to keep a house of yours? Maintain some control over your good name.)

Timeliness of Payments

Very few architects are in a position to, in effect, lend their clients money, or "bank" for them. So architects should provide their services in a prompt manner, bill regularly (usually monthly) and promptly, and be paid promptly. Tell clients in advance, and make sure your policy works for them. The agreement should state clearly that payments due to the architect must be made within x days of submission of statements for services, and if they are not, services will be stopped, the architect will not be responsible for resulting delays and costs, and there will be an additional cost to start up again, as well as interest and fees on late payments. If a client doesn't pay in timely fashion, act accordingly. The phone company doesn't give its customers service for long without payment; neither should architects.

Initial Payment

The signing of an owner/architect agreement should be accompanied by an agreed-upon *initial minimum payment*, to be credited to the owner's account on the last statement for the architect's services. This arrangement allows the architect to work for the length of the project from the owner's capital, rather than using the firm's reserves to cover costs between the start of work on a project and when (typically four to eight weeks later) it in effect is reimbursed for those expenses. An initial payment also serves as protection: should there be a fee dispute, the architect has some of the owner's funds to cover the disputed items.

8   Owner/Contractor Agreements and Contractors' Services

This chapter covers forms of agreements and services between owners and contractors from their point of view rather than from the architect's, although the responsibilities and obligations obviously should be coordinated between the two agreements (owner/contractor and owner/architect), covering the actions of all three parties.

In the discussion of the front end of the project manual (see chapter 5) I suggested that the bid package sent to each contractor include the proposed form of contract between the owner and the contractor, including the general conditions, and the supplementary conditions of that agreement, so contractors preparing a bid know what services they are expected to provide and under what terms and conditions. These issues help define costs of both work and risk for the contractor. In the discussion of the contract administration phase, I described the services that architects provide to owners while the project is under construction.

Forms of Agreement

The appropriate form of owner/contractor agreement, like that of the owner/architect agreement, depends on the size and complexity of the project and the nature of the specific owner, contractor, and architect. The AIA A101 Owner/Contractor Agreement (the fill-in-the-blanks contract itself) and AIA A201 General Conditions (the general

terms of the contract) work together and have the same advantages as the AIA B141 Owner/Architect Agreement: they are court-tested and refined and revised every so often to reflect changes in court decisions and practice so they are current and relevant. They are carefully coordinated with each other, so obligations, rights, and remedies among the parties are consistent between the owner/architect agreement and the owner/contractor agreement; and the agreements are generally considered to be fair to all parties. These attributes make the documents industry standards.

For very small projects a simplified owner/contractor agreement may be in order. Large, sophisticated owners may have their own standard agreements and require that those documents be used. Highly complex, multiphased, or fast-tracked jobs call for other forms of agreement.

The standard AIA A101/201 agreement for design-bid-build projects is a *stipulated sum sole prime general contract*. "Stipulated sum" means the work that is clearly defined in the contract documents is being done for a fixed, agreed-upon amount of money. What it ends up costing the contractor is the contractor's business: if the contractor makes money on the job, the owner can't ask for a refund; if the contractor loses money, the owner can't be billed for more. "Sole prime" means the owner is entering into one agreement for all the work. This agreement is the "general contract."

The basic agreement, or contract ("agreement" sounds so much friendlier, more cooperative, and less contentious than "contract," doesn't it?), such as the AIA A101, contains the names and addresses of the parties to the agreement (the owner and the contractor); the name and address of the architect; a description of the project; the contract sum (the basic price for all the work); a list of the unit prices, alternates, and allowances; the schedule; special terms; and a list of all the rest of the documents, which collectively form the contract documents. Each document is listed by name, with original and latest revision dates; because documents are often being revised and updated, it is important to know which version describes the work related to the stated contract sum. As the work changes, so does the contract sum; therefore the specific original and revision date of each of the documents is necessary to form the baseline. In addition to the basic contract, the general conditions, and the supplementary conditions, the contract documents usually include the working drawings, the project manual, and any bid addenda issued during the bid period.

The rules of the road for the execution of the agreement are spelled out under the General Conditions (A201), which covers not only who does what but what should be done if they don't do what they are supposed to do, also known as "remedies." While the AIA A201 General Conditions is the standard, the AIA also provides somewhat different versions for other project-delivery variations, some of which are described in chapter 4: for federal government projects, multiple prime contract agreements, phased construction, interiors projects, and projects in which the contractor is intended to do work different from what contractors normally do ("revised responsibility" agreements).

An architect experienced in contract preparation can prepare the first draft of the owner/contractor agreement for the project by filling in the blanks in a form such as the AIA A101 and adding any special provisions for the project. The owner's and contractor's attorneys, who are expert in construction contract law and issues (and are rarely the general-purpose family or corporate attorney, no matter how trusted or able) should review the full agreement, particularly if standard forms are substantively modified or if the project has unusual conditions or requirements. The owner and the contractor pay for this legal work. If the architect is not familiar with these agreements, the owner's construction attorney should take the lead.

Summarized on the following page are some of the basic issues in the General Conditions portion of an agreement, such as the AIA A201, which describes the terms and conditions under which a contractor does the construction work. Again, there are many other forms of agreement and conditions that are used in construction.

General Provisions

The General Provisions section of a standard General Conditions section of an agreement includes several concepts that apply to the entire agreement:

1. The contract documents are defined as those listed in the agreement when it is first signed as well as others (such as change orders and related drawings and specifications) that may be added later. The later additions, when agreed to by all parties, become as much a part of the contract documents as items included from the start.

2. If a piece of work or a requirement is defined or described in one place, the concept of correlation and intent establishes that it is as if it were mentioned in all places. For example, if a marble saddle is shown on the drawings at the entry to a bathroom, but there is no technical section about stone or marble in the project manual, the contractor is still obligated to provide the marble saddle. Correlation and intent helps to produce contract documents that are succinct, not repetitious.

3. The organization of drawings and information does not determine who the contractor should engage to do any particular part of the work. For example, if you include some ceramic tile work in a drawing that primarily shows architectural woodwork (cabinet-work), it doesn't mean you are suggesting that the woodworker should do tile work. Which subcontractor or mechanic executes the work is entirely the contractor's decision and responsibility, no matter where in your documents you show that work.

4. Although ownership of documents is primarily an issue between the owner and the architect (see chapter 7, under "Instruments of Service and Copyright Law"), the ownership is stated in the owner/contractor agreement as well. Why? Unless ownership was ceded in the owner/architect agreement, the contractor is notified that the architect's documents cannot be used for other purposes; the owner can't give or sell them to the contractor.

The Owner

The owner is responsible for providing the information about the site (legal, geotechnical, and so on) and for payments required by governmental authorities, such as building department filing fees. Because the contractor in effect extends credit to the owner under their agreement (the contractor does the work; the owner pays periodically for the work done), the contractor has the right to ask for evidence that the owner has the money for the project, either in hand or committed by a lender. Owners don't love having contractors examine their financial wherewithal, but this issue of privacy versus risk is their business.

The owner and contractor agree, consistent with the owner/architect agreement, that all communication between the owner and the contractor will be through the architect. From the owner's point of view, this arrangement keeps the architect liable. From the architect's point of view, it helps avoid decisions being made without full information and professional input, and thus helps protect the owner and the public.

Finally, the owner has the right to stop the work and to correct and complete it without the contractor if the contractor fails to do the work or doesn't correct defects in the work after receiving proper notice.

The Contractor

Consistent with the contractor's obligations in the bidding process, as stated in the instructions to bidders (see chapter 5, under "Construction Documents"), the contractor affirms that all the documents have been thoroughly reviewed and that any errors or omissions discovered in the documents will be promptly reported to the architect. The contractor is responsible for providing labor, materials, supervision by a competent superintendent, management, and direction to complete all the work, including construction means and methods (see chapter 5, under "Contract Administration"). The contractor agrees to

1. keep and update the project schedule;

2. obtain all required submittals, review them for conformance with the contract documents (a requirement not often rigorously followed), submit them to the architect, and revise and resubmit them if required;

3. keep a full set of documents and submittals (shop drawings, samples, schedules, and product description sheets, known as cuts) on site (so the architect need not carry all that stuff on every site visit);

4. keep the site clean;

5. indemnify (provide protection) against personal or property damage caused by the work;

6. provide all required cutting and patching.

"What?" you ask. Why is cutting and patching of the thousands of pieces of construction that the contractor has to do mentioned in the owner/contractor agreement? I don't know. Tradition? History? The fact that it is not spelled out anywhere else, and it does need to be done? Chalk it up as one of the many oddities of the construction world.

It is the contractor's obligation to conform to and comply with the requirements of the contract documents: to build what is shown and described, in the quantity and quality indicated in the contract documents. Remember: it is the architect's obligation to endeavor to protect the owner from any failure of the contractor to do the job, but that is a much lesser obligation than the contractor's, which is to *do it.*

Contract Administration

Though not a party to the owner/contractor agreement, the architect is listed in it and plays a critical role acknowledged by the other parties. The owner/contractor agreement defines the extent of the architect's role as agent and representative of the owner and specifies if it is other than standard. If the role of and services by the architect are to be different from those described in the owner/architect agreement, those other roles and services must be agreed to by the architect and the owner. The description of roles and services in the AIA A201 matches those in the AIA B141 Owner/Architect Agreement. In any case, both the owner and the contractor have the right to expect that the architect will administer the owner/contractor agreement fairly and evenhandedly, showing partiality to neither party. The architect should

1. handle all communications between the owner and the contractor, as all parties have agreed;

2. review and certify the requisitions, or applications for payment, submitted by the contractor;

3. prepare change orders and construction change directives;

4. conduct observations and inspections.

The architect has the right to reject any construction not in conformance with the contract documents and is wise to advise the owner of any such work, even if the architect thinks such nonconforming work should be accepted.

If there is a dispute between the owner and the contractor, either of them should bring the disagreement (in writing) to the attention of the architect, whose duty is to examine the circumstances and issue a written finding, or opinion. If either party doesn't accept this first line of dispute resolution, the matter can then be taken to the American Arbitration Association for nonbinding mediation, and if that fails, for binding arbitration. If mediation and arbitration are deleted from the agreement, disputes are settled in court.

Finally, the owner and contractor agree to waive any claims for consequential damages.

Subcontractors

At the beginning of the project, the contractor must submit to the owner a list of all proposed subcontractors. If a proposed sub does not meet a requirement that was stated in the relevant technical section of the project manual, the contractor must select and propose an alternate sub that *does* meet the requirements, at no additional cost to the owner. If the sub meets the spec requirement but the owner rejects the sub for another reason (such as pending litigation between the owner and the sub, or prior bad experience with the sub), the contractor must replace the rejected sub. If the replacement sub costs more, the owner must pay the additional cost, after approving it.

Subcontractors are hired by and in the employ of the contractor, who is responsible for them. All communications to the subs go through the contractor.

Work by Owner or by Separate Contractors

If, before execution of the owner/contractor agreement, it is expected that some of the work on the project will be done by contractors or subcontractors outside the terms of the owner/contractor agreement, prior notice that the owner intends to utilize such **separate forces** should be given during the bid period, because it may affect the contractor's bid and schedule.

For example, if an owner has a longstanding relationship with an architectural woodworker or cabinetmaker and wishes to hire her or him directly (not through the contractor) to install bookshelves while the contractor is still working on the site, the owner may do so on the understanding that the owner, the contractor, and such separate forces hired by directly by the owner will cooperate with one other regarding access to the work, protecting previously done work and protecting work after it has been completed. The owner/contractor agreement calls for this mutual respect and responsibility.

If the contractor fails to meet the requirements of the agreement, the owner has the right to hire separate forces directly to do the work.

Changes in the Work

There are many reasons for changes in the construction of a project. The owner's needs may evolve (sometimes a polite way of saying the owner's program was wrong); the architect may see a mistake in the design or think of a better way to do something; the contractor may want to substitute materials or find **developed field conditions** or **unforeseen conditions**–for example, a wall slated to be demolished in a renovation project is opened up and buried within are found the main electrical lines for all the floors above: time for Plan B. Although changes almost always wreak havoc on the schedule, the scope, and the budget of a job, sometimes they are unavoidable.

Changes should be dealt with as follows:

1. The architect defines the scope of the work thoroughly and clearly (what work is being added and what is being deleted) and provides clear drawings (known as construction sketches, or CSKs) and, if necessary, revised specifications, for the portion being changed. Consultants may advise, if appropriate. The architect submits this information to the contractor as a notice of proposed change (NPC).

2. The contractor and appropriate subs prepare a proposed change order (PCO) describing the work, including, if applicable, changes to the contract sum based on previously agreed-upon unit prices, and to the schedule, in days to be added or subtracted.

3. The architect reviews the contractor's PCO and may request further explanation or revision to make the PCO acceptable. (If the PCO cannot be agreed on, see step 5.)

4. The architect prepares a change order (CO) including the scope of the work and revised contract sum and schedule. The architect, the contractor, and the owner sign the change order, which now becomes a part of the contract documents.

5. In the event a proposal acceptable to the owner and the contractor cannot be achieved (usually because the architect and the owner think the price is too high or the delay too long), the architect prepares a construction change directive (CCD), which orders the contractor to proceed with the change for a stated (or to be determined) sum. The CCD is signed by the architect and the owner and becomes a part of the contract documents. The contractor then must proceed with the work, even if not in agreement with the cost and time adjustments. This arrangement prevents contractors from exacting an unreasonable extra charge from the owner just to keep the job rolling.

6. The contractor makes the change.

Time

The owner/contractor agreement states the time within which the contractor must complete the work, known, unsurprisingly, as the *contract time*. The contractor prepares, at the start of the work, a schedule that shows when each stage of the work will be completed and lists milestones for the project; for example, the foundations will be completed by May 15, the steel erection will be completed by August 1, and the building will be enclosed and weather-tight by December 1. The contract time can be changed by mutual agreement of the architect, the owner, and the contractor by a change order or by agreement of the architect and owner with a construction change directive, as described above. There may be agreed-upon remedies in case the contractor falls behind or does not meet the milestones—for example, weekend or overtime work programs at no added cost to the owner. The architect is responsible for monitoring the schedule, but it is the contractor's responsibility to meet it.

If the contractor fails to adhere to the contract time, the owner/contractor agreement may specify a *liquidated damages* remedy, which calls for the contractor to pay (or have deducted from the contract sum) a predetermined amount, often assessed per day, representing the actual cost to the owner of the contractor's lateness. A second, alternate arrangement is a *bonus-and-penalty* clause, which awards the contractor a set amount of money per day if the work is finished early and penalizes the contractor if it is finished after the stipulated date. Some states require a bonus clause to accompany a penalty clause; in other states a penalty clause is not permitted at all.

Either a liquidated damages or a bonus-and-penalty clause may cause the contractor to focus unduly on causes for delay, and the owner and architect may spend a lot of time dealing with the contractor's claims. For example, if enough money is at stake, the contractor might issue an extraordinary (and perhaps wholly unnecessary) number of RFIs (see chapter 5) to support a claim that the work couldn't reasonably be done on time.

A contractor-requested change in contract time may also result when other parties don't fulfill their obligations (for example, the owner does not give timely answers or payment, or the architect does not process submittals or answer reasonable questions in a timely manner) or when circumstances beyond the control of the parties occur—strikes, "acts of God" such as hurricanes, tornadoes, or floods, or acts of terror, all collectively called *force majeure*. In these cases, the contractor may reasonably be entitled to a delay claim, an extension to the contract time, and perhaps an increase in the contract sum to cover the added general conditions for extension of the job.

Payments and Completion

As explained in chapter 5, the amount, per agreement, adjusted during the course of the work by change order or by construction change directive, that the owner owes the contractor for the work is the contract sum. It is divided into parts, usually for each trade, for change orders, for general conditions (the contractor's job-related costs for the superintendent, laborers, rubbish removal, and on-site office expenses), for overhead (the project's share of the contractor's general business expenses, such as rent and office staff), and for profit (yes, contractors deserve to make a profit). Insurance costs, which used to be included in the general conditions and overhead as part of the costs of doing business, became so large an expense during the very tight market of the 1980s that it is often now listed as a separate item. This breakdown of the contract sum is often based on the bid breakdown part of the bid form, agreed on at the start of the work. It is known as a *schedule of values* for requisitioning purposes. In a stipulated sum agreement (when the contractor agrees to do a clearly defined scope of work for a set price), the schedule of values is not a representation that these amounts are the contractor's actual costs for each of the subs. In private bid jobs, this is confidential information and none of the owner's business. But the scheduled amounts should, in the architect's reasonable professional judgment, generally represent what each trade is worth.

The contractor makes *application for payment* at specified intervals, typically monthly. The application includes a *certificate of payment*, or requisition cover form, and the *continuation sheet*, which shows the details of the requisition by line item, including the agreed-upon schedule of values, any approved change orders, the work covered in previous requisitions, the work covered by and through the current requisition period (as dollar amounts and percentages of completion, used by the architect in evaluating the req), the amount of work remaining to be done, and the retainage.

Retainage, perhaps 10 percent of each item, is held by the owner until completion of the project. For example, if the electrical work on a project has a total scheduled value of $100,000, when the electrical work is 30 percent completed the contractor gets $27,000 from the owner to pay the electrical sub: ($100,000 x 30%) - ($100,000 x 30% x 10%). The retainage may, under the agreement, be reduced at the halfway mark of the project or at substantial completion (see below). Retainage is the stick to get the contractor to finish the punchlist, the tool to cover defaults.

If the req covers any materials stored off-site, it should include proof, such as paid invoices from suppliers, passing title to the owner. Typically, the architect has seven days to review and act on the req. The architect may deduct for work not done properly or for "over-req'ing." The owner is obligated to pay the amount approved by the architect within seven days after the architect's action (that is, by the fourteenth day after the contractor submits the application to the architect). If the contractor does not receive payment on time, the contractor is entitled to send a default notice to the owner saying that without a "cure"—that is, payment by day 21—work will stop and the owner may not make a claim for delay.

Substantial completion, which must be certified by the architect, is the time at which the project is sufficiently complete to be used for its intended purposes. Substantial completion triggers a number of contractual issues. At substantial completion retainage may be reduced, giving the contractor a big chunk of money; the contractor's standard one-year warranty period begins at this time. Contractors therefore want the architect to certify substantial completion at the earliest possible time. The owner/contractor agreement provides that if the work is not really substantially complete but, because it is late, the owner must begin to occupy it, such occupancy whether full or partial may not necessarily mean that substantial completion has occurred.

To achieve *final completion*, the contractor must have fulfilled all contractual obligations (except warranty-period work, if any). The contractor achieves final completion on completing the punchlist, producing final waivers of liens from all subs, suppliers, and the contractor itself; and delivering all manuals, certificates of compliance, final certificates of occupancy, sign-offs, "as-built" drawings, if required, and warranties. The architect monitors receipt of these items and issues a *certificate of final completion*. The architect helps produce a *close-out reconciliation* of monies between the owner and the contractor by adjusting the final contract sum for allowance and contingency balances, contract savings, unresolved change orders, value of owner acceptance of nonconforming work, bonuses, penalties or liquidated damages, and any deductions to the contract sum for additional costs to the owner caused by changes in services caused by contractor defaults.

Protection of Persons and Property

It is the contractor's obligation to provide a safe job site: creating, implementing, and enforcing a safety program to protect property and persons on and near the job site. The contractor must be aware of and conform to all safety requirements at the local, state, and federal levels, and handle emergencies on or around the site. If any hazardous materials (asbestos, radon, and the like) are discovered on the site, the contractor is responsible for notifying the owner, who must remove them.

Some large contractors (and even owners) have safety officers to ensure compliance with regulations and keeping the construction site safe.

Insurance and Bonds

Both the owner and the contractor should get expert advice and carefully review the details of insurance for each project. (Insurance for architects is discussed in chapter 10.) Obviously the owner should ensure that all relevant risks are covered to the extent necessary or desirable, in the owner's business judgment, and that risks are not left uncovered on either party's policy or redundantly covered on both parties' policies. Usually owners insure against losses to their property and to construction work that they have paid for, while contractors insure against losses for damage to property or persons caused by their work, for their tools and equipment, and for completed work not yet paid for by the owner. Typically workers hurt on a job are covered by state-mandated *workers' compensation*. *Project policies* that cover all aspects of a project (including the architect's risks) are sometimes available.

Bonds purchased from insurance companies (*sureties*) can cover some risks to the owner. Before construction, the risk that a bidding contractor won't enter into an agreement for the bid is covered by a *bid bond*, as discussed in chapter 5. Bonds also can cover two of the most serious risks during construction—the contractor's failure to finish the project because of bankruptcy or for any other reason; and the contractor's failure to pay the subs or vendors for work or materials the owner has paid for, causing the subs or vendors to file a claim (a *lien*) against the owner's property for payment. The first risk can be covered by a *performance bond*; in the case of a default, the surety providing the bond pays for any additional costs the owner incurs by having other contractors complete the work. A *payment bond* (previously known as a *labor and materials bond*) covers the second kind of risk to an owner: claims made by unpaid subs or vendors.

For a contractor to be "bondable," insurance companies examine the history, reputation, and finances of the contracting company very carefully. Often contractors' personal assets are used as collateral to the surety for providing bonds, giving contractors a serious disincentive for defaulting. The very fact that a construction company is bondable gives some owners a certain level of security and comfort, even if they don't actually buy any bonds (which are an owner's additional cost). If someone is willing to stand up for that contractor, the contractor is probably okay, the thinking goes.

Uncovering and Correcting Work

If the architect wants to inspect portions of construction before they are hidden from view by subsequent work (for instance, to check pipes in a wall before the wall is finished and closed, or back-caulking on a fixed light window before the trim is applied), the contractor should be alerted to the request in advance of completion of that work (always in writing—the spoken word doesn't count) so the contractor can notify the architect when to make the inspection. If a contractor fails to give such notice to the architect, the contractor must uncover the work (open and re-close the wall) at no additional cost to the owner. If the architect doesn't request an inspection but has good reason to suspect something has been done wrong and concealed, the architect can request that the work be uncovered (the wall opened) for inspection. If the work turns out to have been done correctly, the contractor can charge the owner for the uncovering. If it was done incorrectly, the contractor must correct the faulty work and pay for the operation. It's a good idea for the architect to discuss a request for uncovering and potential additional cost with the owner before making the request to the contractor. (A sharp owner will ask the obvious question: Why didn't you ask to inspect before the work was covered up, so that I wouldn't be faced with a potential "extra"? Good question.)

Sometimes an owner may elect to accept nonconforming work—work not done per the contract documents—or a punchlist left partly incomplete. As an incentive the contractor may offer a reduction in the contract sum. Whether or not the owner agrees is the owner's business decision, to the extent that it doesn't affect public health and safety.

Finally, note that it is in this section of the General Conditions (the topic of most of this chapter) that the general one-year warranty on the contractor's work is covered. Exceptions to the one-year period are discussed in the section of chapter 5 about the technical sections of the project manual.

Miscellaneous Provisions

Miscellaneous provisions cover a variety of issues that do not deserve their own sections in the standard General Conditions.

If an owner is located (by residence if an individual, by place of business if a company or institution) in one state and the project is located in another, which state's laws cover the contract? The state in which the project is located. The answer is important, because most contract issues are governed by state contract law. Owner/architect agreements, in contrast, are covered by the state of the principal place of business of the architect. This issue becomes important in regard to joinder issues.

Can the owner/contractor agreement be passed on ("assigned," in legal language) to successors? Yes, but with the same obligations and with the consent of the other party.

When must claims for damages be made? Usually within twenty-one days of finding the circumstance or problem. Dawdling is inadvisable—and if someone does, it may be a way to sidestep a claim.

Who pays for tests not required in the contract documents? The owner, if the work passes the tests; the contractor, if it fails.

Contract Termination

Should either the owner or the contractor substantively fail to fulfill its obligations, the agreement can be unilaterally ended. Specifically, if the owner puts a project on hold for more than thirty days or doesn't cure a nonpayment default notice from the contractor, the contractor can terminate the agreement and obligations under it. Similarly, if the contractor fails to execute the work or to correct work not properly done, the owner can, with proper notice to the contractor and opportunity to cure, terminate the agreement. The party at fault often pays a penalty to the terminating party.

Alternate Owner/Contractor Agreements

The standard owner/contractor agreement described at the beginning of this chapter as a "stipulated sum sole prime general contract" assumes a full set of contract documents that are complete, or at least sufficient to describe the scope of work being purchased by the owner at the time of entering into the agreement and to set a fixed price for that fixed scope of work. Unfortunately, life isn't always so clear and simple. There are alternative arrangements, some of which are discussed in chapter 4—such as construction management, fast tracking, and design-build. Each arrangement requires a different form of agreement between the owner and contractor, as well as between the owner and architect, to cover the terms and conditions that are appropriate and relevant to those circumstances.

When construction has to begin before all the drawings are done, the contractor may charge the owner for the actual costs (of labor, materials, and subcontractors), adding overhead and profit either as an agreed-upon percentage of the costs to be reimbursed or as a fixed amount. This arrangement is called *cost plus* or *cost plus a fee*. Sometimes after the drawings are completed, the owner may elect to have the contractor do the work on a cost-plus basis, perhaps to a maximum price, known as a *guaranteed maximum price* (GMP). Other methods of compensation may be used: if the owner rather than the contractor signs the agreements with the subcontractors, the contractor is actually a construction manager rather than a contractor per se.

Whatever contracting arrangement is used, it should be appropriate for the specific project, be clearly described in the agreement, and be clearly understood by all parties. Every arrangement has different responsibilities, obligations, and risks that should be carefully evaluated. If the owner/contractor arrangement is changed after the owner/architect agreement is signed, that agreement (and the architect's fee) should be modified accordingly.

9 The Architect's Office

This chapter considers the architect as an entity—that is, the architect's firm—and the main issues you must understand to run a firm successfully. This information is useful whether you work in someone else's firm or start and run one of your own.

Starting a Practice

Regardless of the reasons you decide to start a firm, you face many decisions and new issues. In fact, one of the most exciting aspects of running a firm is the range of topics to learn and master, making it a perfect job for people who enjoy being the ultimate generalist, as many architects do.

If you think you want to go out on your own, revisit the questions I asked you in chapters 1 and 3: what are your personal values, your strengths, your expertise and interests? These are qualities that will make you and your firm unique. They shape how you go about attracting and keeping staff and clients.

Many studies of professionals and firms group them into categories defined by core values, services, and the kinds of clients they are likely to attract (and hence should probably market to). While each study has its own "take," most highlight:

1. Expertise. The prime feature offered by expert firms is new ideas, typically unusual or highly personal. This group includes the celebrity architects, known for their design talents and flair. The likely clients for this type of firm are those for whom a unique, special design is critical to the success of their project.

2. Experience. Some firms offer particular know-how: in building types (for example, hospitals), geography (for example, the Southwest), or systems types (for example, prefab or modular construction). Such firms have honed their skills in these areas, which are sometimes quite complex. Clients who want to play it safe go to a firm that has done many of "their" type of building before; they may not get an earth-shattering or unusual design, but it will work as intended.

3. Execution. Sometimes the hardest part is getting it done. Projects that are very large, in a difficult place to build, on a tough schedule or budget, or have other special requirements that would confound the average professional need a firm that can deliver under these conditions. Such firms specialize in processes and procedures. Building a new hospital in an underdeveloped country in three months is not a project the average architect can deliver.

While it may be convenient to try to sort firms into these three categories, really great firms succeed at all three; they provide great design flawlessly executed with innovation, thoroughness, and integrity. Every firm should aspire to do this.

Another way to look at firms is by their operating values. Some firms are what might be called "practice-centered." Architecture is a way of life for the firm's members, who live and breathe architecture 24/7; doing it as well as possible, until whatever hour, is what drives them. Other firms are "business-centered"—the practice is a livelihood and the members consider it primarily as a business rather than a mission. These two characterizations are of course extremes; the best firms, for the long haul, combine some of both of these virtues (and, unfortunately, vices).

Whichever way you slice it, a critical component of running a firm is the integration of values, market, technology, and focus. These must coordinate and "fit" with staff and clients. Ultimately firms are people working together, and their goals, beliefs, and values must harmonize. It is essential to know yourself, your staff and colleagues, and your clients. Lack of fit hurts all involved.

Forms of Ownership

Every firm is a legal entity, whether it comprises one person or several hundred. The form of the entity is governed by the laws of the state in which it is located. While laws vary from state to state, most offer three options for ownership and organization. Because architecture firms are also covered by the state's licensing laws, the options differ somewhat from the options for other kinds of business. The states regulate the permitted business form; the Internal Revenue Service defines business types for tax-filing purposes.

1. A *sole proprietorship* has one owner, who is liable professionally and financially for everything the firm does. A sole proprietor may work alone or have any number of employees. For tax purposes the income and expenses of a sole proprietorship are considered part of the sole proprietor's personal tax filing. The business expenses of the firm, including employees' salaries, are entered as expenses on the sole proprietor's tax return. (The sole proprietor's personal checkbook and the firm's checkbook could be the same, but I wouldn't recommend it. Keep two checking accounts and two sets of records, even if you are the firm.) Typically, sole proprietorships are small firms, but there are some with many employees. Sole proprietorships are the simplest form of practice to start and run, but they have limitations, notably the inability to share ownership and risk.

2. A *partnership* is owned by two or more partners. Most very large architecture firms have partners numbering in the dozens (other types of professional partnership, such as those of accountants and lawyers, sometimes have hundreds, even thousands, of partners). Partners may share ownership equally or unequally. An important feature of partnerships is the "joint and several liability" of the partners, which means that each partner is liable for actions of every other partner, to the full extent of each partner's personal assets, not just for that partner's share of the partnership. If you are one of six partners and the firm is sued and judged at fault with a monetary judgment awarded to the claimant, and you are the only partner with personal assets, to the extent the judgment exceeds the assets of the firm, you are liable to pay that judgment. (In other words, only go into a partnership with people you know very well and trust entirely.) A partnership files a partnership tax return; the profit (or loss) for the whole firm is apportioned to each partner according to that partner's percentage share of the partnership.

   3. A *professional corporation* is a company owned by its stockholders. Many large firms are owned and organized this way. Although it has the most legal requirements for operations, which may make it expensive or cumbersome for a small firm, it simplifies the process of adding and removing owners. In some circumstances the personal assets of the firm's owners can be shielded from the firm's business liabilities (such as paying rent). However, the owners' assets are not protected from liabilities caused by their actions as professionals, such as designing a building that falls down and hurts someone.

   Some states permit *limited liability partnerships* (LLPs) and *limited liability corporations* (LLCs). These alternate business formats can shield the owners from liabilities of a business nature but not from professional wrongdoing. A limited liability partnership may also reduce the level of joint liability of some partners if they were unaware of wrongdoing by one partner.

   Most states permit only licensed design professionals to be owners of architecture firms, no matter what the form of the firm. Some states permit licensed engineers or licensed landscape architects to be owners in architecture firms, so long as one (or, sometimes, a majority) of the owners is a licensed architect. Almost always, the owners are all personally liable for professional errors or omissions, or *malpractice*. Personal liability is considered part of the compact with society for being a licensed professional. ("Professional" in this context differs substantively from the broader, colloquial definition discussed in chapter 1.)

   Before selecting the form of ownership for a firm, you should consult a knowledgeable attorney and an accountant, who can help you select the format that is most appropriate and beneficial for your circumstances and ensure that all legal requirements are met.

Staffing a Firm

Unless you plan to practice alone—a satisfactory arrangement for some, very lonely for others, out of the question with any sizable amount of work—you will need to find, maintain, train, and encourage the people who work with you. I use the word "with" rather than "for" intentionally. A firm is *all* the people who work in it, not just the owners. The quality of the work and the success of the firm are directly related to the quality of the staff. In small firms, everyone does a wide variety of tasks. In large firms, personnel are trained for more specific, limited roles, but they must also receive broader training to advance and grow.

Large firms tend to organize their staff in one of three ways. The **horizontal**, or **departmental**, **method** divides a firm into departments, such as "design," "production," "field." Each department carries out one portion of every project: the design department does the schematic and design development of all the firm's projects; the production department produces all the working drawings and specifications; the field department handles all the construction administration. Projects move through the various departments.

The **vertical**, or **project**, **method** of organization divides the staff into project teams; each team handles its projects from beginning to end.

The horizontal method has the advantage of greater staff expertise at each type of task, but it loses the continuity and the "thread" of how, in a specific project, a programmatic issue became a design solution and therefore how a related problem should be resolved in the field, with the memory and knowledge of *why* it is *how* it is. The vertical form of organization has the flip-side pros and cons: the project team has continuous knowledge of all the issues of its project and a deep commitment to the project, but the team members may lack the depth of expertise and experience of how to best perform each phase of service.

A hybrid arrangement, which combines the best of the horizontal and vertical methods, is called the **matrix method**. Here each project has team leaders who are involved from beginning to end, but the team is assisted in each phase by office specialists who join (and leave) the team as needed. This format is best for larger offices, depending on the particular office's history and culture. Some large offices divide into "studios," which (besides sounding very artistic) combine great horsepower and scale, for marketing and management reasons, with more manageable working groups whose members feel they play a significant part. Studios may be organized by building types—the office-building studio, the educational-facilities studio, the housing studio—or by specialty—the historic-buildings studio or even the small-projects studio.

Whatever the size and organization of a firm, the owners must handle seven key situations as described below:

1. *Hiring*. Find the best and most suitable employees. Good sources (to keep in mind when looking for a job as well as when trying to fill one for your firm) include your friends, former classmates, friends of your employees, and students (yours, your employees', or your friends'). The wider the net, the better! The skills, experience, personality, and character of these candidates are known; you can judge their suitability for employment much better than that of candidates you meet through a want ad, job listing, or school job fair, whom you must assess only through an interview and the references you check. When you offer a candidate a position, you should describe the responsibilities, compensation, benefits, and other terms of employment, preferably in writing. A simple letter will serve. Employment contracts are not common except for very senior positions.

2. Personnel policies. It is fair, and indeed is sometimes a legal and insurance requirement, to give all employees an **employees' manual**, a document that clearly states the firm's employment policies: the criteria for advancement and dismissal; holidays observed, vacation, personal, and sick time; maternity leave; health and other benefits; compensation; and office standards of practice. When policies change, inform the staff in writing. A loose-leaf format is convenient for updating.

3. Delegation of responsibilities and authority. Never assume that employees intuitively know what is expected of them. Be explicit and clear about what they should and should not do in as many circumstances as you can reasonably predict. To the extent possible, authority (what a person is permitted to be in charge of) should be commensurate with responsibility (what he or she will be held liable for). For example, is the employee authorized to make direct contact with clients? With contractors? By whom must his or her work be reviewed before it is sent out? To whom does the employee report?

4. Motivation. Finding good people is hard; keeping them motivated, energized, excited, focused, and productive is harder. The success of a firm depends on everyone doing their best—and this is vital for their own satisfaction and reward. Like finding clients whose goals coincide with the firm's, the concordance of goals, values, and mission of everyone in the firm, owners and employees, is key to a constructive and happy workplace (and life).

5. Evaluation. Good managers meet periodically with employees, discuss their strengths and weaknesses, and offer suggestions for improvement. They listen carefully to their employees' views about their work, projects, colleagues, goals, and desires for change. No matter how well you think you know your staff, you may learn a surprising amount from listening and heeding.

6. Compensation. Architects may be more mission-driven than money-driven compared to other professionals, but we cannot escape the fact that our society largely measures success by economic reward and that living a good life requires a certain amount of money. Some architecture firms offer unpaid internships. I firmly believe this practice is unprofessional and immoral. It is also illegal. (This country *does* have a minimum wage law, after all.) While working should always be an educational experience, an architect's office is not chartered as an educational institution, and asking someone to pay "tuition" by having them provide unpaid work is totally wrong and anathema to everything the profession should be and should stand for. No other profession treats its "young" this way. It is corrosive, abusive, and a bad part of architecture culture, and it leads to worse behavior later in one's professional life, such as working for inadequate fees. Employees may be paid either a salary–$x per week–or by the hour–that is, $y per hour for the hours worked, with time over a given number, say forty hours, at either "straight time" (the same rate as below the forty hours), which is common for professional workers, or at "time and a half" for overtime (that is, 1.5 times the rate for the forty hours per week), which is normal for clerical and support staff.

7. ***Employees or consultants?*** Firms often hire outsiders as "consultants"–engineers, cost consultants, even architects. The consultants may be individuals or firms, who offer expertise in some area. This is legitimate and proper. Some employers, though, with willing employees as co-conspirators, offer ***employment*** on a consulting basis. This arrangement can reduce the employer's obligations to pay municipal, state, and federal withholding and employment taxes as well as unemployment and workers' compensation insurance premiums. Employees called consultants can take home a check without all those pesky deductions and can claim certain expenses as business deductions for tax purposes, which would not be allowable deductions for employees. This may sound appealing, but the IRS has very clear rules distinguishing a "consultant" from an "employee." If your employer tells you what to do and how to do it; if you work for your employer primarily in the employer's office; and if you spend most of your working time working for that employer and not for others, you are an employee, not a consultant. (After all, calling yourself a dentist doesn't make you a dentist.) In the long term such abuse hurts both the employer and the employee: the employer, by creating potential exposure for fraud, back unpaid taxes, and employee liabilities; the employee, by lost opportunities for coverage of risks such as on-the-job injury and unemployment, and tax liabilities long after receipt of payment or services. As with all abuses, everyone suffers in the end.

The Workplace

Almost by definition, architects believe in the importance of the physical environment and in the positive effect it can provide its inhabitants. The workplaces of architects are often their clearest statement to the world, in tangible terms, of their beliefs and values and their skill in using resources wisely, efficiently, and tastefully. In other words, your office probably says more about you as a professional than doctors' or lawyers' offices do about them. Your office does not have to be lavish; indeed, that can scare clients, who might think your fees will be commensurate or wonder how it expresses your hierarchy of values. Great offices may range from well-laid-out rooms in your own home, to spacious quarters taking up many floors of an office building.

When our firm was relatively small (about fifteen people), we had a sun-filled, cheerful suite with a great view. One client told us we won the job because the office of their first choice was so dark and depressing that despite that firm's great reputation, the client couldn't bear the idea of going there for meetings every week. An inviting workplace is one way that H. H. Richardson never mentioned to get (or lose) a project.

At the other end of the spectrum were the offices of the firm I worked for the summers I was in architecture school. They occupied three floors of a Park Avenue building in midtown New York City. The walls of the conference rooms facing the lobby reception area (furnished with Barcelona chairs) were clad in floor-to-ceiling slabs of dark green Antique Verde marble. Facing the beautifully detailed stairs connecting the floors hung a large Aubusson tapestry. The studios were open, spacious, and light-filled, with low partitions between the drafting tables (two decades before CAD). The statement the office made to the clients and staff was one of quiet grandeur, elegance, and strength—all entirely appropriate for the firm.

The point is: suit the size and décor of the office, whether it is a small startup or a larger firm, to its needs and clientele; plan for human work comfort, changing technology, and staff interaction; include space for storage (samples, reference books, files, and drawings, which will exist for a while longer). And space for a good coffeemaker. An architecture office should be practical and expressive, not so expensive that paying for it is a burden. Remember that too fancy can be as much of a business hazard as too plain.

10 Insurance, Legal, and Accounting Matters

Insurance Issues

All kinds of insurance, whether car insurance or professional liability insurance, operate on the same basis. The fundamental concept of insurance is the pooling or sharing of risks. It is a transfer of risk from an individual or firm to an insurance company (also called a *carrier*) that covers a group of such risks. Many individuals or firms pay a relatively small amount each year–the *insurance premium*–to share in the ability to collect larger sums of money should something unpredictable (and usually bad) happen to them. The maximum amount recoverable from the company that collects and redistributes the money is called the *coverage*. Insurance companies evaluate the risk of each potential insured and, through a process called *underwriting*, determine the cost of carrying that risk. The insurance company's agreement with the insured is called a *policy*; the company collects the premiums from the policyholder, the insured, and invests the funds for safekeeping and for investment income. When a policyholder suffers an *event*–a loss against which the policy insures–the policyholder makes a *claim* to the insurance company. If the insurer finds the claim is for a *covered event*, it pays the policyholder for the loss. Usually, to help reduce the cost of the premiums, insurance policies include a *deductible*, an amount the policyholder pays. Thus the insurance company pays the loss up to the coverage amount, less the deductible.

General Business Insurance

Architects face many risks and should consider insurance to protect against them. All businesses face the possibility of loss to their property, typically the office and its contents (furniture, furnishings, computer equipment, and the like), by fire, theft, flood, and vandalism. In addition, architects might insure valuable documents (of course our drawings are valuable!). These cannot simply be replaced, like desks and chairs. Liability insurance covers accidents–for example, a client slips in the office, falls, and is hurt. Both property and liability coverage are offered by insurance companies as *multi-peril business owner's policies*, also known as BOP (and not at all related to Charlie Parker), or *commercial general liability insurance* (CGL). These policies do not cover acts of professional wrongdoing, which is discussed below.

Business interruption insurance, as its name implies, covers continuing fixed expenses, lost profit, and even temporary or permanent relocation costs if your business is prevented from operating because of fire, explosion, hurricane, or collapse. Most business owners also insure their employees against certain risks. State and federal laws require workers' compensation, which covers an employee's injury on the job (in most states employees can't sue their employers for such losses), and also unemployment insurance. Elective forms of insurance to benefit employees include health, dental, disability, and life insurance. (Other non-insurance benefits that employers may provide their employees include retirement plans, 401-K tax-deferred savings plans, and profit-sharing plans.)

Construction and Professional Insurance

A second group of risks—ones that are specific to the construction world—are covered by bonds—bid bonds, performance bonds, and payment bonds (discussed in chapters 5 and 8). In addition, owners often require **contractor's insurance**. **Project insurance**, covering all the risks and liabilities for all parties of a project, is also available. Insurance advisors advise owners and contractors on these options.

Last but hardly least is **architect's professional liability insurance**, which covers a firm's past and present employees and owners for claims and claim adjustment expenses (mainly lawyers' fees, which can sometimes be very large, even in excess of the actual claim) arising from suits for negligent acts, errors, and omissions in their performance of professional services. (This insurance is sometimes colloquially known as E&O insurance, for errors and omissions.) Claims can be brought against design professionals not only by those with whom they have agreements, typically owners, but also by others, known as **third parties**, who might be adversely affected by a professional's negligence (for example, a passerby falls on a wet, slippery sidewalk designed by an architect). Insurance brokers and attorneys who are expert in this specialized field can advise architects on professional liability insurance. A limited number of carriers provide this coverage, and they vary somewhat from year to year as companies enter and leave the field. It's customary for architecture firms to complete applications for several carriers to obtain competing quotations, or bids. Before giving you quotations for coverage, all insurance companies require you to complete lengthy questionnaires designed to tell their underwriting department about the degree of risk you represent. The key information includes the firm's history of lawsuits and judgments, the scale of the firm (judged by its gross volume of fees billed and the construction put in place in past, current, and projected future years), the kind of work that the firm does (some building types, such as dams, nuclear plants, bridges, and condominiums, attract more lawsuits than others), and the form of project delivery most frequently used for the firm's work (design-bid-build and fast-track projects historically produce more disputes than the other project delivery methods covered in chapter 4). Additional considerations are the ratio of owners to employees, licensed to nonlicensed staff, stability of size, use of standard AIA documents as opposed to owners' agreements, and consistency of clientele. Finally, insurers ask if the applicant is aware of any circumstances that could lead to suits. This must be answered accurately, because although disclosure of potential upcoming problems might cause the insurance company to charge higher premiums (or refuse coverage), discovery of lack of full disclosure may permit the insurance company to deny coverage of a claim.

The overall risk or exposure of each firm, together with the amount of coverage it seeks (which is often described both "per occurrence" in a given year, and "aggregate" for all occurrences in a given year), and the amount of loss it is willing to self-insure (its deductible), determine the insurance premium.

Architects' professional liability insurance is usually only available on a *claims made basis*, which means that the insurance company picks up the loss when the claim is made, not as with most general insurance, when the fault occurs (*occurrence basis*). For example, if I designed a project in 2004, it was built in 2005, it leaked in 2006 because I designed it incorrectly, and the owner makes a claim (sues me) in 2007, the insurance company that is carrying my professional liability insurance in 2007 is the carrier that handles (and pays for) the claim, even if other companies carried my insurance in 2004, 2005, and 2006. An important corollary to claims-made-basis policies is that they cover *prior acts*—that is, services you performed before the current policy period are covered by the current policy. Such "practice" policies cover the work done by the firm. In contrast, the project policy mentioned in chapter 8 is typically paid for by the owner and covers all parties involved in the project. The advantage of the project policy for the architect is that it excludes all risks associated with that project from the firm's professional liability policy, thereby lowering subsequent practice policy premium costs. Project policies have the advantage to the owner of ensuring continued coverage, reducing costs of claims among those covered, and covering joint defense costs in third-party suits.

If you run a firm and decide to retire, how do you protect yourself from claims made in the future for work done in the past? Buy a policy with a "tail," which covers claims after you no longer practice.

I said earlier that professional liability policies cover claims made arising from an architect's professional services. What don't these policies cover? Typically they exclude warranties and guarantees (which is why it's important not to make them), general business non-professional issues that are covered by business owners' policies and workers' compensation, business obligations (such as paying rent or consultants), fraud or criminal acts, clients who don't pay their bills, and certain services relating to hazardous materials (*hazmats*). Coverage and exclusions vary among carriers, and policies should be carefully compared with the help of experienced insurance advisors and attorneys for your firm's specific needs.

Some firms elect not to purchase insurance for certain risks and *self-insure* for them instead. Just as the deductible is the self-insured portion of a covered (insured) risk, not insuring at all for a given risk is being self-insured for that entire risk.

Legal Issues

Legal issues flow through virtually every aspect of practice. Contract matters are covered in chapters 5, 7, and 8. Firm ownership and employment practices are discussed in chapter 9. Issues relating to public constraints are discussed in chapter 12. Here I cover issues relating to negligence and antitrust.

Legal obligations are incurred in three ways. By **contract**, one party promises another party to do (or not do) certain things. By **statute**, local, state, and the federal government, through their legislative and administrative branches, pass laws and make regulations. Finally, by **common law**, precedents and decisions of courts at all levels create obligations.

The statutes (laws and regulations) affecting architects enacted by the federal government include copyrights, OSHA regulations, taxes, unemployment insurance, and antitrust. The states regulate contracts, professional licensing, business rules, forms of ownership, workers' compensation, unemployment insurance, statutes of limitations for claims, and taxes. Municipalities—cities and towns—administer zoning, building codes, business taxes, and landmarks.

Architects are expected to act in a professional manner and exercise a reasonable **standard of care**, normally judged (in general, by society; specifically, in a lawsuit, by a judge or jury in court or by an arbitrator in arbitration) to be "what a reasonably prudent architect would do, in the same time and place, given the same or similar facts and circumstances." Whether or not the architect met the appropriate standard of care for a given situation is usually determined (normally in the context of a lawsuit) by testimony of expert witnesses, which defines the architect's legal duties and rights. Some owner/architect agreements call for more than a normal standard of care. An architect's obligations can be increased by promising in an agreement to do more: if an agreement calls for providing "services to the very highest professional level" or "the very best possible professional services," the bar rises substantially and the architect may be more likely in a dispute to be found not to have done what was promised. Indeed, many professional liability policies do not cover such a situation. So it is critical to show your attorney and insurance carrier any proposed deviations from standard agreements to be sure those clauses are insurable. (Telling clients in a negotiation that the clause they want to add to or delete from the owner/architect agreement would render your professional liability insurance policy void will often make them rethink how badly they really want that clause.) As noted earlier, warranties, guarantees, and certain promises, such as providing a higher than normal standard of care or an unachievable schedule for performing professional services, can also be uninsurable. *You are not required to provide perfection*, only a reasonable standard of care. You are permitted to make mistakes, just not mistakes beyond what a reasonably prudent architect would make in a similar situation. Unless you promise more, that is.

Anyone can sue you at any time, but that doesn't mean they can win.

To be successful in a suit for professional negligence against an architect, the suing party (the plaintiff) must prove four things:

1. **Duty.** The architect had a legal obligation to do (or not do) something. This obligation may derive from the owner/architect agreement, from statute, or from precedent. It normally includes providing a reasonable standard of care (unless, of course, you promised more, making it your duty to provide whatever level of care you promised).

2. **Breach.** The architect failed—by action (such as giving instructions to the contractor, without authorization from the owner, to proceed with work that increased the contract sum); by error (doing something wrong, such as specifying a roofing product inappropriate for the project's climate); or by omission (not doing something that should have been done, such as providing sufficient details for a roofing project)—to perform the duty.

3. **Cause.** The breach of the duty is the proximate cause of harm to the plaintiff.

4. **Damage.** Actual harm, or damage, occurred as a result.

The plaintiff may be the owner or a third party, such as a passerby or neighbor to whom the architect owed professionally sound services. In some jurisdictions a *statute of repose* provides a time limit on the right of a plaintiff to bring an action. The beginning of the time limit, or *trigger date*, may be either substantial completion or when the potential problem was observed (vague and hence undesirable). There are also *statutes of limitations*, which define the time limit after the date of an injury or damage for bringing a claim.

In the construction world claims are usually either for *design errors*, in which case the problem arises from improper design, or for *construction errors*, in which the actual work was not built according to the plans and specifications and the variance is the cause of the damage. Architects are responsible for design errors, contractors for construction errors. In reality it is sometimes difficult to assign the cause of the problem, but as noted in chapter 7, most agreements prohibit joinder, which would allow an owner to bring a single action against both the architect and the contractor, in essence saying, "I've got a problem. I don't know (or care) whose fault it is; I just want you both to pay." Assigning fault for a problem is critical to solving it and is required when joinder is prohibited.

Remember the case of the office building with a leaking deck, described in chapter 7 (see page 87)? Sometime after it was done, we heard from the owners that they were experiencing some leaks below the roof deck. We inspected it, made some recommendations to fix it, and heard nothing else for over a year, when they sued us and the contractor together. Here is some of what was deficient in how they brought the lawsuit, and how these defects in their suit persuaded them to take a more reasonable approach to solving the problem. Our attorney and our insurance carrier reviewed the owner/architect and owner/contractor agreements and notified the owner that because both prohibited joinder, separate actions against architect and contractor would be necessary. Thus the owner had to determine whether the problem resulted from a design error (sue the architect) or a construction error (sue the contractor). The owner couldn't simply say there was a problem that was someone's fault and ask the court to figure out whether it was the architect or the contractor. Moreover, the agreements called for arbitration, which would be in different states because architect's principal place of business (the location for the owner's suit against architect) and the project (the location for the owner's suit against the contractor) were not in the same state. Given these conditions, the owner agreed to the amicable resolution in which four parties (owner, contractor, architect, roofing sub) shared a simple repair. The moral: if a problem can be solved by everyone working together and sharing the burden, it is much better than running to your corner, calling in the lawyers, and filing a lawsuit.

Architects, owners, and contractors face risks in any project. Risks should be evaluated by their probability of occurrence and for the severity of the possible outcome, or loss. In general, it is fair to assign the risk to the party most able to control that aspect of the project. Architects accept the risk of design errors; contractors, the risks of cost and time overruns and construction errors; owners, the risk of an unsuccessful outcome from a business point of view. Each party must evaluate whether the potential reward is sufficient for the risk undertaken, and how much of (and at what cost) the risk can be transferred to an insurer. Controlling risks means identifying them in advance, taking steps to reduce the likelihood of their occurrence, responding quickly and appropriately if they do occur, and doing what is possible to reduce or mitigate their damage. An architect accepting a project must decide if the fee is sufficient for the risks that might arise. The fee must cover the time necessary to produce a thorough set of documents, to check them carefully, and to spend sufficient time on submittals and in the field during construction. These steps are necessary to reduce risk.

Architects may reduce their exposure by including in their agreements clauses that limit their liability to a set amount of money, perhaps the value of their fee, regardless of the magnitude of the loss, or by limiting the periods for asserting claims with a "trigger date." Such provisions must be consistent with the specific state's laws to be enforceable and do not reduce the architect's exposure to claims from third parties who were not part of the agreement.

Some owners' agreements include *indemnification*, or "hold harmless," clauses, in which one party agrees to pay for the liabilities of another party—a transfer of liability and an acceptance of risk. Guess from whom and to whom the risk is usually being transferred? Such provisions should be reviewed by the architect's attorney and insurance carrier. Even if they are not uninsurable, if they bring on additional risk, there should be commensurate additional compensation.

Antitrust is the last legal issue to consider. How, you may wonder, does antitrust relate to architects? Antitrust laws say that it is illegal (1) to fix or maintain prices, (2) to boycott a competitor or customer, or (3) to allocate business or customers. Any agreement between two or more parties that unreasonably restrains trade is illegal. The AIA fee schedule that set the minimum fees permitted to be charged by architects who were members of the AIA was in violation of point #1 (see chapter 6). If two architects agree not to work for a particular client, they are in violation of #2. And if a number of firms get together and divide up work—this project is mine, that one is yours—they are in violation of #3. Conspiracy to break the law, even if it fails, is still breaking the law. You are not permitted to discuss fees with your colleagues, who in theory should be competitors, even if setting reasonable fees is of mutual concern, nor to discuss what you might charge a potential client, even if hundreds of architects are competing for the project. It is *not* illegal, though, to talk history: you can discuss what you charged for work in the past.

In the 1980s the New York Chapter of the AIA tried to deal with the issue of poor compensation and proposed that firms pay starting architects an agreed-upon starting salary. Considering the paltry amount they were paid, the idea hardly seemed radical. The U.S. Department of Justice's Antitrust Division thought otherwise, considering it a clear violation of the Consent Decree the AIA had signed in the 1970s when it banished the Minimum Fee Schedule and promised not to promulgate anticompetitive measures again. The Justice Department felt the AIA/NYC's idea of setting starting salaries (which would have rippled up to affect all salaries) was an agreement among firms that were supposed to be competitors to fix a major component of architects' fees, namely salaries. Another Consent Decree was signed, including a requirement to educate and sensitize young architects about the issue. Which is what I'm trying to do here.

Accounting Issues

Chapter 11 discusses how to make money on a project; covered here are the basic accounting concepts that permit you to obtain an accurate picture of your firm's finances. These concepts apply to (and are necessary for) firms of any size—one person to five hundred people—though obviously large firms utilize more sophisticated tools as well. There are two basic economic issues: the flow of money in and out over a given period of time, and the value or worth of the firm at any one point in time.

Money coming in is known as *income*; that going out as *expenses*. These are captured on an *income and expense statement* (see fig. 10.1) for a specified period, such as a month, a quarter, or a year. The statement may be historical or a projection of the future. Typical income for an architect's office includes fees for professional services, reimbursable expenses, rental income (if you sublet some of your space or property), and investment income. Expenses usually include salaries, payroll- and other salary-related taxes and costs, fees paid to consultants, rent, telephone, leases for equipment (such as copiers and computers), insurance premiums, postage, delivery services, interest on loans, purchases of equipment and software, information services, and subscriptions. If income is greater than expenses, the difference is *profit*; if income is less than expenses, the difference is *loss*; hence the income and expense statement is sometimes called

INCOME AND EXPENSE STATEMENT	LEE MILLER ARCHITECTURE
January 1, 2006 through December 31, 2006	1771 S Central Ave Phoenix AZ 85004 602.345.3344 www.lma.pro

INCOME

Fees	$550,000.00
Reimbursables	$8,500.00
Desk Rental	$4,500.00
Interest on Bank Account	$375.00
TOTAL INCOME	**$563,375.00**

EXPENSES

Salaries	$254,000.00
Health Insurance	$17,000.00
Professional Liability Insurance	$12,000.00
General Business Insurance	$2,500.00
Legal Fees	$2,500.00
Accounting Fees	$6,000.00
Telephone	$3,500.00
Rent	$32,000.00
New Equipment	$6,000.00
Equipment Repairs	$1,500.00
Copier Lease	$2,400.00
TOTAL EXPENSES	**$339,400.00**

PROFIT	**$223,975.00**

Partners' Draw	$200,000.00
Increase Cash-on-hand	$23,975.00

10.1 Sample income and expense statement for a year of a small firm with two partners, whose salaries ("draws") are the profit. Not shown here are some tax-related issues, such as depreciation on their equipment.

a *profit and loss statement* (P&L).

Expenses may be divided further into *direct expenses*, which are attributable to specific projects, and *indirect expenses*, which are the costs of running an office (overhead). For example, the portion of salaries paid for time spent on projects is allocated to each of those projects as direct expenses, while the portions spent on vacations, sick leave, office work, and holidays are indirect expenses.

Income and expenses can be considered either as happening when the obligations occur, called accounting on an *accrual basis*, or when the actual transactions occur, called accounting on a *cash basis*. If, on October 31, you send a client a statement for services, and you receive a check and deposit it in November, on an accrual basis it is income in October; on a cash basis it is income in November. (Checks can be used on a cash basis, and no, this is not the same as keeping two sets of books—it is simply two different ways of keeping track of transactions.) Professional services firms report their income and expenses on a cash basis for tax purposes. Cash basis accounting is also necessary to provide information to manage a firm's cash flow, so that on payroll day you actually have the money in the bank to pay your staff. In the larger picture, or on a more "macro" scale, the accrual basis is more useful for telling you how you are doing financially—what your income and expenses are over the longer term.

While income and expense statements are analogous to a movie of a certain duration, another view of a firm's finances is like a snapshot at a given moment, such as the last day of a year or half-year. This view looks at all the things of value a firm has at that time (its assets)—cash in the bank accounts; what clients or others owe (*accounts receivable* or AR); the value of equipment (such as computers and furniture); office improvements made; real estate holdings; and any other investments. Against these are set all the firm's obligations (*liabilities*)—taxes due; what is owed to employees, consultants, suppliers, and vendors (called *accounts payable* or AP); and any loans outstanding. The schedule of the two columns is an *asset and liability statement*. The difference between assets and liabilities is a firm's *net worth*, or value (see fig. 10.2). Realistically, architecture firms (indeed, most professional services firms of any sort) do not have great net worth. To quote my father, at service firms "the inventory goes down in the elevator every night."

For a small to medium-size firm, a good general-purpose accountant who is familiar with professional service businesses will be satisfactory. You don't need an accountant who specializes in architecture firms. The accountant can help strategize the best format for a given practice, guide it through the relevant regulatory and tax issues and reporting requirements, assist in keeping the books, and maintain compliance with all appropriate governmental agencies. Good, reasonably priced software packages such as Intuit's QuickBooks or QuickBooks Pro should supplement the accountant's input and can

ASSET AND LIABILITY STATEMENT

as of December 31, 2006

LEE MILLER ARCHITECTURE
1771 S Central Ave
Phoenix AZ 85004
602.345.3344

www.lma.pro

ASSETS

Cash-on-hand	$32,000.00
Accounts Receivable	$45,500.00
Equipment	$9,000.00
Furniture	$4,000.00
TOTAL ASSETS	**$90,500.00**

LIABILITIES

Accounts Payable	$18,000.00
Equipment Loan Balance	$7,800.00
TOTAL LIABILITIES	**$25,800.00**

NET WORTH	**$64,700.00**

10.2 Sample asset and liability statement for a small firm.

help keep small and medium-size firms' records, on both cash and accrual bases. Such programs can produce income and expense statements, create P&Ls, and even project-track staff time and expenses. They keep track of accounts payable and accounts receivable, and they make most financial aspects of office management considerably simpler than in the precomputer past.

I don't know anyone who chooses architecture as a profession for the fun of keeping the books. But accurate and up-to-date records let you know where you are financially and help you make projects and the business profitable. And profit helps a firm do better design—by giving you the time to hone designs so they are as good as you can make them; to document them well so they are built as you intended, efficiently, and with as little friction as possible; to attract, train, and keep a great staff; to afford the premises and equipment to help you do your best work; to have the resources to weather slow times; and to be able to market the business and help get the best projects you can.

11 Project Management

A project is a planned undertaking. It starts with a need, followed by a plan to meet that need, and the implementation to realize the plan. An architectural project is both the design and the built manifestation of that design. (Sometimes unbuilt designs are called projects, but here I use the word in its fuller, constructed and realized sense.) Project management is the series of considerations and actions that get projects realized. Although architects have always practiced project management, it is only in the last fifty years that it has been given a name. The complexity of the effort required to get something designed and built has increased so much in this time span that it requires special skills, expertise, and tools. Independent consultants (and firms) now offer these skills to clients, but I believe that except in the most complex and difficult projects, the architect is best equipped to serve effectively as the project manager.

Every building project begins with an owner or client who wants something built. The first task of project management is to define the task clearly, including not only the complete program but also the budget, the schedule, and the resources that will be used to accomplish the task. Then the project manager (who may be the owner, the architect, a third party, or a member of any of those parties) assembles the team to do it. In the design-bid-build method of project delivery, this team is usually chosen in stages over time: first the architect, then the consultants who work for the architect, then the contractor. In other project delivery systems the team is put together in different orders.

Project Schedule

Once the task has been clearly stated and agreed upon, and the team assembly begun, the project manager prepares a schedule of the steps needed to realize the project. The schedule can be expressed in many different ways. For a very simple project, such as a small house addition, it might just list the date of completion of each of the steps—a "milestone list" as illustrated in figure 11.1. An expanded schedule, like that shown in figure 11.2, combines the time schedule of each task with the architect's projected staffing, hours, and billing rates, showing the architect's fee related to each task. This provides the owner and architect with a cash flow projection for fees for professional services for the duration of the project. A slightly more complex schedule used for medium-sized projects is a bar chart, also known as a Gantt chart, illustrated in figure 11.3 for the same project. This schedule has the time (in days, weeks, or months, depending on the project) across the top, a list of tasks, and bars showing when each task is to be done (often color-coded to show by whom it will be done). This format obviously gives more information than the milestone list, but it still doesn't clearly show the

Preliminary Schedule of Work

May 1, 2006

Work	Start	End
Set design direction, document existing conditions	8.25.06	9.29.06
Design all major components	10.2.06	10.31.06
Prepare filing set & complete design details	11.1.06	12.1.06
Complete construction documents	12.4.06	2.28.07
Bidding/negotiation of construction contract	3.1.07	3.30.07
Order long lead items, contractor mobilization	4.2.07	4.30.07
DoB filing and approval	12.1.06	3.30.07
Construction phase	5.1.07	10.31.07

Preliminary Schedule of Work and Budget of Architects' Fees

May 1, 2006

Work	Start	End	Staff	Hrs	at	Cost	TOTAL
Set design direction, document existing conditions	8.25.06	9.29.06	KD	40	165	$6,600	
			PR	100	100	$10,000	
			MK	75	75	$5,625	
							$22,225
Design all major components	10.2.06	10.31.06	KD	40	165	$6,600	
			PR	150	100	$15,000	
			MK	150	75	$11,250	
			SD	150	85	$12,750	
							$45,600
Prepare filing set & complete design details	11.1.06	12.1.06	KD	25	165	$4,125	
			PR	150	100	$15,000	
			MK	150	75	$11,250	
			SD	150	85	$12,750	
							$43,125
Complete construction documents	12.4.06	2.28.07	KD	50	165	$8,250	
			PR	300	100	$30,000	
			MK	450	75	$33,750	
							$72,000
Bidding/negotiation of construction contract	3.1.07	3.30.07	KD	10	165	$1,650	
			PR	100	100	$10,000	
							$11,650
Order long lead items, contractor mobilization	4.2.07	4.30.07	PR	30	100	$3,000	
							$3,000
DoB filing and approval	12.1.06	3.30.07					
Construction phase	5.1.07	10.31.07	KD	40	165	$6,600	
			PR	240	100	$24,000	
							$30,600
							$228,200

11.1 A sample simple project schedule, showing tasks to be done and a related schedule. In this case the tasks do not correspond to the normal five phases of services (though they are included). This represents custom-tailoring the scope to the specific needs of the project.

11.2 The same simple project schedule showing tasks to be done with the related schedule, projected staff time required, and the resulting fee.

#	Task	Precedent	Duration	Start	Finish	Staff	2006 JUL AUG SEP OCT NOV DEC	2007 JAN FEB MAR APR MAY JUN JUL AUG SEP OCT NOV DEC
1	Set design direction, document existing conditions		26 days	8/25/06	9/29/06	KD, PR, MK	8/25 ☐ 9/29	
2	Design all major components	1	1.1 mos	10/2/06	10/31/06	KD, PR, MK, SD	10/2 ☐ 10/31	
3	Prepare filing set & complete design details	2	1.1 mos	11/1/06	12/1/06	KD, PR, MK, SD	11/1 ☐ 12/1	
4	Complete construction documents	3	3.2 mos	12/4/06	2/28/07	KD, PR, MK	12/4 ☐ 2/28	
5	Bidding/negotiation of construction contract	4	1 mo	3/1/07	3/30/07	KD, PR		3/1 ☐ 3/30
6	Order long lead items, contractor mobilization	5	1.05 mos	4/2/07	4/30/06	PR		4/2 ☐ 4/30
7	DoB filing and approval	3	4.3 mos	12/1/06	3/30/07		12/1 ☐ 3/30	
8	Construction Phase	6, 7	6.55 mos	5/1/07	10/31/07	KD, PR		5/1 ☐ 10/31

11.3 The project schedule in Gantt chart form.

#	Task	Precedent	Duration	Start	Finish	Staff	2006 JUL AUG SEP OCT NOV DEC	2007 JAN FEB MAR APR MAY JUN JUL AUG SEP OCT NOV DEC
1	Set design direction, document existing conditions		26 days	8/25/06	9/29/06	KD, PR, MK	8/25 ☐ 9/29	
2	Design all major components	1	1.1 mos	10/2/06	10/31/06	KD, PR, MK, SD	10/2 ☐ 10/31	
3	Prepare filing set & complete design details	2	1.1 mos	11/1/06	12/1/06	KD, PR, MK, SD	11/1 ☐ 12/1	
4	Complete construction documents	3	3.2 mos	12/4/06	2/28/07	KD, PR, MK	12/4 ☐ 2/28	
5	Bidding/negotiation of construction contract	4	1 mo	3/1/07	3/30/07	KD, PR		3/1 ☐ 3/30
6	Order long lead items, contractor mobilization	5	1.05 mos	4/2/07	4/30/06	PR		4/2 ☐ 4/30
7	DoB filing and approval	3	4.3 mos	12/1/06	3/30/07		12/1 ☐ 3/30	
8	Construction Phase	6, 7	6.55 mos	5/1/07	10/31/07	KD, PR		5/1 ☐ 10/31

11.4 The project schedule on a CPM chart.

relationship of the tasks. For this, the more sophisticated Critical Path Method (CPM) or PERT chart, illustrated in figure 11.4, is needed. Although it looks something like a bar chart, the CPM adds an important level of information: what specific tasks need to be done for each other task to start. This line is expressed as the "critical path" and shows what steps need to be done faster to speed completion of the project. Adding resources to accelerate those steps causes the critical path to shift, showing other tasks for possible expedited treatment.

Scheduling enables all the parties involved in the project to agree on each party's role—what they are to do and when they have to get it done. It helps each party, whether an individual or a firm, to make its resources available when needed. It is also the tool by which the project manager monitors the various stages of a project to ensure that each one is done on schedule. If a task is not done on schedule, the project manager can deploy a remedial or catch-up program, such as working overtime or adding staff or shifts. Alternatively, the duration of the project can be extended (commonly known as "being late"—not popular with owners).

Project-management software packages, such as Microsoft Project, are available at reasonable cost; are easy to learn to use; allow the project manager to easily prepare, modify, and update sophisticated schedules; and assist in easily developing alternative, "what-if" scenarios.

Project Organization

Project management also encompasses procedural matters that are critical to the success of a project. As with goals, design, schedule, and budget, the parties must agree on management style. In the *hub-and-spoke method*, all communications flow through one central party that makes all decisions. In the standard AIA owner/architect and owner/contractor agreements, all parties agree that communications will be through the architect, who agrees to keep the owner informed. While this looks like the classic hub-and-spoke with the architect as the hub, it is not the most effective way of running any but the smallest projects. What's better? A process in which more people share information through regular project meetings where all parties (or their representatives) hear all the issues and discuss solutions to the problems that inevitably arise. If everyone participates, the project and the parties all benefit. All receive relevant information and views at the appropriate time and understand how decisions were arrived at. Participation reduces conflict flowing from "I didn't know that" and "someone should have asked what I thought." It remains critical for all information to flow in an agreed-upon and orderly, well-recorded protocol. The information is documented by meeting minutes, memos, e-mails, or other written records.

When everyone works as a team with common goals and the desire to work problems out together, projects run more smoothly and are likely to be more profitable for all than when the parties are adversarial. A formal process called **partnering** encourages team-work and helps prevent disputes by means of workshops and team-building sessions, sometimes organized by outside facilitators, hired by the owner or jointly by the owner, architect, and contractor. Project insurance offers another, somewhat indirect method of reducing disputes. Finally, other methods being tried in other countries actually reward, with substantial monetary bonuses, all parties involved in projects that get done well, on time, on budget, and without disputes. Friction on a job hurts everyone—financially, psychically, and professionally. When our New York-based firm opened a branch office in Seattle, we found the people involved in our projects there all shared in the desire to do high-quality work as efficiently and painlessly as possible. The work was better, more profitable, and more fun. We applied what we learned and became much more selective about the clients and the contractors we worked with back east, and we found the results to be similar. We worked hard to develop more repeat clients with whom we had lasting relationships, with the result that the majority of our projects now are for clients for whom we previously worked. One client, with whom we've done many projects over the last decade, insists on using the same team for each new project: architect, engineers, contractors, and subcontractors. This client actively promotes good team interaction and hosts regular (and very enjoyable) team outings and events. There is never finger-pointing or dispute. The work is very high quality, and it is economically rewarding and effective for everyone involved.

Effective project management requires focus and discipline. It is necessary not only to *know* the right way to handle all the steps, but to *do* them accurately and methodically, from the beginning of the project to the end. Communicate through the proper channels. Document all information clearly and thoroughly, so someone looking at the records years later can understand exactly what happened. File and store documentation so it is easily retrievable. It is critical in an office to store information—sketches, drawings, letters, e-mails, notes, and telephone logs—in files that are logical and consistent from one job to another. If everyone in the office keeps records for each project labeled and filed differently, no one else can find things. Digital storage has certainly made this easier.

Project Budgeting

Good project management controls all aspects of a project—its quality, duration, and cost. In general, it is easiest for the owner and the architect to make effective and meaningful adjustments to the budget for the construction cost in the schematic design phase, when scope and quality are still in the embryonic stage. During the bid phase, cost adjustments can be made by the prudent use of alternates. It is very hard to make budget changes during construction (short of major cuts in the project.) Budgets for escalation and contingencies should exist for every stage.

Major variation in cost can be caused by the complexity or unusual nature of a project. Contractors love to build what they are familiar with and usually charge a very large premium for designs that are unfamiliar (and therefore scary) to them. Design factors such as size, shape, height, space efficiency, systems, and quality of materials all have substantial cost implications. Location can influence cost in terms of climate, ease of construction, labor rates, degree of unionization of the local work force, proximity to labor and materials, and availability of well-managed contractors. Site-specific factors such as soil-bearing capacity, need for rock removal, drainage capacity for rain and septic systems, availability of utilities, and stringency of local code and zoning regulations also affect cost.

Under normal agreements the architect is responsible for ascertaining that the program and budget "fit." Never start a project thinking that a budget that is undersized for the program requirements will work out and that you'll be lucky in the bid process. Maybe you will, but I wouldn't count on it. I've never known it to happen.

At every stage of your work, you must provide the owner with budget updates and confirmations, as explained in chapter 5.

Remember: these are your best professional judgments, not guarantees. Many architects are qualified to provide owners with such nonstandard services as a *detailed quantity take-off*, which lists the exact quantity, by count, square footage, linear footage, and so on of every item of construction; a *detailed cost estimate*, which inventories the quantities and applies appropriate market costs per unit (unit costs); and *life-cycle cost analysis*, which determines the real cost of a building over its useful lifetime. It takes into account not only the original cost (of construction, land, and fees) but also the costs of financing, operation, and maintenance (including expected energy costs), as well as repair and replacement costs. These are adjusted to present value by estimating future interest costs and taking into consideration the timing of the actual costs. Through life-cycle analysis the owner can make better-informed decisions, for example, choosing to pay higher initial construction costs for more energy-efficient components to reduce future annual energy costs, producing savings that will create a total overall lower cost over the building's lifetime.

Who Does Project Management for a Client?

Architecture is a complex discipline; architects learn to break down big problems into smaller, more digestible problems and find compatible solutions to each. We have to orchestrate and coordinate the efforts of many allied disciplines, such as engineers and other consultants on their parts of the project. While many project management consultants market their services, usually as owners' representatives, to owners, very few of them can offer the breadth and depth of education, expertise, and knowledge that architects have. The most effective project management consultants often have professional training as architects or in an allied field, such as law or engineering.

Others have *not* only not been helpful, but (at huge expense to the owners) have been a real hindrance to the project–they sometimes sell their services to owners on the basis of frightening them with tales of how projects have gone awry, and how they will prevent bad things from happening, even though they bear no liability if problems do occur. They then (perhaps unconsciously, or am I being charitable?) have to create problems to earn their keep. Further, they sometimes stand between the owner and the architect, trying to filter (and control and even distort) the communications between owners and architects. This is a sure way to have a bad project. By and large, unless the project is very complex or difficult, the classic three-party (owner, architect, contractor) process works most clearly, fairly, and effectively. It does rely on the architect being qualified and sufficiently compensated to provide the appropriate and necessary services. It also requires a client with the time and focus to properly fill the owner's role.

Architects' Management of Their Own Services

Project management includes not only running the overall project, but monitoring its progress within the architect's office. To make a project profitable to a firm requires many elements to be in place. The scope of the architect's services must be clearly defined; they must match what the architect is capable of doing, what the project needs, and what the owner expects. The architect's fee must be adequate to provide those services. The architect must perform services in an efficient and effective way and must carefully budget and monitor time and costs for the services for each phase of work. Finally, if any of the expectations are not being met (for example, more services are being provided than are covered by the fee), the architect must become aware of that quickly, must identify the causes, and must remedy them. If problems are due to outside factors (such as client-initiated changes to the program necessitating redesign; or nonperformance by a contractor, requiring the architect to perform additional administrative services), without a fee increase, they must be addressed and corrected. On a small simple project, a work sheet such as the one shown in figure 11.2, listing tasks, schedule and duration, personnel, and rates must be developed in preparation for setting the fee. It can be monitored, recording and comparing "actual time" spent by the architect's staff in each phase to "budgeted time," and corrected as the project proceeds. Larger projects operate in the exact same way, but with more sophisticated software tools for scheduling, planning, and monitoring the professional services budget.

While great design is an essential ingredient to great architecture, successful implementation of that design is equally necessary. The project management skills and effort necessary for high-quality execution are often not fully appreciated by architects or owners.

12 Zoning and Building Codes

While many laws and regulations, such as those concerning licensing, copyright, contracts, and liability, affect the *practice* of architecture, the two sets of governmental controls that most affect the *designs* of buildings are zoning and building codes. *Zoning*, the more "macro" of the two sets of laws, controls the allowed uses and size and shape of a building on a given site and other issues that have an effect on a building's surroundings. *Building codes*, in contrast, deal with more "micro" issues, primarily involving the safety of buildings. Both zoning and building codes may be considered reasonable incursions on the individual rights of property owners for the health, safety, and welfare of the community. The balance between the individual's rights and the public good (or "how much can the government tell me what I can do on property that I own") has been adjusted over the years and continues to be argued and modified by governmental actions and challenges to them in court. The degree of governmental control over private property varies across the country: it is affected by regional differences and responds to differing needs caused by local conditions, from weather to population density to political and social mores.

Usually the states have the authority to impose both zoning and building codes. The states transfer this authority to local governments to enact, administer, and enforce them. While some large cities, such as New York City, historically have written their own zoning and building codes, many municipalities, particularly smaller cities, towns, and villages, choose to adopt standard building codes, either in whole or with minor modifications; sometimes local governments hire consulting firms to help them write or update their zoning codes. These codes take into account the specifics of the area covered but are often based on generic models.

The Architect's Role

At the beginning of any project the architect usually meets with the appropriate person (a building inspector in a small town, a plan examiner in a larger city) in the local building department to learn what zoning, building, and other codes and laws the specific project must conform to. For example, the architect of an apartment house in New York City must design to meet the requirements not only of the city building code and zoning resolution, but also of the New York State Multiple Dwelling Law and federal ADA requirements. You need a current copy of each law or code applicable to your project or access to them online, if available. Even if you know the laws and the area, carefully review the relevant codes for each new project to see which sections apply. (Anyone who told you this would all be simple lied to you.) As your plans develop, meet with the building officials, ask questions, take notes, and review solutions with them. The process can either be efficient or, if improperly managed, painful and costly.

Your responsibility is to create building designs that conform to all applicable codes and to assure the owner and the community that the completed building meets those codes. This is not easy; indeed, sometimes it is not even entirely possible. You may interpret some wording one way; the building inspector, another. Sometimes projects fall under the jurisdiction of more than one authority—for example, the building department, planning and zoning, the fire department, and the highway department. When multiple laws apply, the design must conform to the most restrictive. Studying the codes (that is, reading them many times) and consulting the appropriate building department personnel, other architects familiar with similar projects, and governmental authorities will help you get the job right. Codes and standards of practice change constantly; ongoing, life-long learning is essential.

What happens if you fail to meet code requirements during the design phases? Redesign. During construction? Rebuilding. But remember: the standard of care is not perfection or being 100 percent right 100 percent of the time. See chapter 10 about legal issues.

Zoning

Every local jurisdiction, according to its state's laws, can have a zoning code (or "law" or "resolution"). Statutes (enacted by the legislative branch) and regulations (enacted by the administrative branch) guide and control the physical development of the jurisdiction; they also tie it to desired physical and population density and uses and to the infrastructure of roads, public transportation, utilities, schools, and health facilities to support that development. Villages and towns usually have codes of relatively simple rules that fit in small booklets; the complicated laws of big cities may fill many volumes. Following are the basics, common to almost all zoning codes.

Codes are divided into two parts: map and text. The maps, which may fit on a single page for a small village or extend to fifty or more pages for a large city, show the full area of the jurisdiction and divide it into different zones. Each zone is given a classification, which corresponds to sections of the text portion of the code. In rural areas the zones may be residential segments with differing hierarchical levels (R20, R40, and so on), agricultural zones, and commercial zones. Cities typically include residential, commercial, and manufacturing zones (but no farms). The maps tell you both the name of the zoning segment, or district, of a specific site, useful for learning about that site, and the boundaries of a particular zoning classification, useful for looking for areas that apply to rules in the text.

The text of a zoning code usually begins with a section on administration, which states what the law covers and how it is administered (proposals examined and laws enforced). Next, often, comes a section of definitions of technical terms, which sometimes have meanings that are different from or more specific than the same words' meanings in common English usage. The definitions clarify, for purposes of interpreting law, how the terms are used—for example, distinguishing between a "basement" and a "cellar."

Most zoning codes then specify what is permitted in each zoning classification segment or district shown on the map. They include a list of all the imaginable uses, from single-family residential use to slaughterhouses and tanneries (obviously, some codes were written a long time ago). Uses range from benign (for example, low-density residential use) to noxious (for example, heavy industry), in terms of the traffic, noise, and pollution they may generate, and sometimes the uses are graded with use-classification numbers on a scale from least to most noxious. The text then correlates the uses and the mapped zones to indicate what uses can be located in which zones—that is, what are the *permitted uses* for each zoning district. In older cities zoning codes were written after the cities were well established, and the first zoning maps were drawn to generally organize the permitted uses relative to what was already there. Always, the basic goal of a well-thought-out map is to take into account the history of the area (the existing building types and uses), its physical features (topography, waterways, views), its man-made attributes (utilities, services, roads, and mass transit), and the local government's planning goals,

which may encourage growth in certain areas and limit it in others. A typical goal is to prevent the adjacency or proximity of very different uses—for example, keeping new factories out of established residential areas. Well-planned areas usually have gradations of uses over the area—for example, houses next to retail next to light manufacturing next to heavy manufacturing, but not houses next to heavy manufacturing.

In addition to use, the code text covers *bulk*—the allowed sizes and shapes of buildings and the placement of buildings on sites. Bulk regulations control the future density of development of each part of the jurisdiction in terms of population and building area (and the resulting stimulus to growth and demand on infrastructure), as well as the possible reduction of sunlight and air that are available to adjacent private sites and public ways that would be caused by future development.

Size typically is controlled in two ways. First, the maximum allowable floor area for a given location is usually defined as its maximum allowable *floor area ratio*, or FAR, the ratio of the floor area of a building to the area of the lot on which the building is located. The FAR, ranging from a fraction to 20 or more, is the basis of calculating the maximum area you can build on a given site. It is obtained by multiplying the maximum permitted FAR by the size of the lot. (For example, on a 50' x 100' site, with a permitted FAR of 3, you can build 50 x 100 x 3 square feet of floor area, or 15,000 square feet.) The number of floors that area can (or must) be distributed on is determined by the permitted shape of the building. The law may provide different maximum FARs for a given site depending on the intended use of the building—thus it might permit *x* FAR for a residential building and *y* FAR for a school. Sometimes laws permit extra, or bonus, FAR, if in the development of a site the owner provides special features that are not required but of benefit to the community. Such incentive zoning can encourage civic improvements. In a big, dense city bonus FAR might be given to an owner for providing on-site entrances to a subway to replace sidewalk entrances that cause congestion; in return for giving up valuable ground-floor space for the subway entrance, the owner is permitted extra square feet of floor area on upper floors.

The second set of rules that determine the size of a building are its *height and setback* requirements, which also affect its *shape*. As with FAR, the permitted height and required setbacks vary by zoning district and correlate to the map. Height requirements may be defined simply as the allowable number of feet or stories. (Consult the definitions section of the code to see what it means by height. Is it to the top of a pitched roof? The ceiling of the top floor? Is there a difference between "floor" and "story"? What is a "mezzanine"?) The rules can also add levels of complexity by, for example, relating the permitted height to the context—proximity to the site's boundaries or to existing adjacent buildings.

Building setbacks control the appearance of bulk and help give more light to the ground near the building. Setback requirements may prevent building walls that go straight up above a certain point, mandating, say, that after a building facade wall is 85 feet high, there must be a horizontal setback of at least 10 feet horizontally (in plan) before the wall can rise higher. Zoning may also require a wall over a given height to step back within an imaginary plane (sometimes known as a *sky exposure plane*) of a given angle, or pitch—for example, 1 foot back horizontally for every 4 feet up. Building setback requirements are common in densely populated locations.

Zoning can control how a building is set on its site by several different sets of requirements. A limitation on *lot coverage*, the portion of the site that is built on and from which you cannot see the sky from the ground plane, is *open space* and is usually expressed as a percentage of the lot size. Lot coverage limitations are most common in areas of relatively low density; high-density urban areas often permit 100 percent lot coverage. Another set of siting limitations require building setbacks on the front, sides, and rear of buildings (often known respectively as front yards, side yards, and rear yards), typically from the site boundaries of the project, to afford privacy, light, and air to the building and to adjacent buildings and public ways (sidewalks and streets).

In addition to the basic use and bulk controls of zoning codes, zoning also specifies requirements for **off-street parking** (often a major factor in suburban commercial or multifamily residential projects) and for **signage** (size, location, and whether illuminated or not). Zoning may also include **design controls**, matters of appearance that contribute to the urban design of an area. For example, cities may require that in selected areas a building's facade be held at the street property line and rise to a certain height—no more, no less—to maintain the overall facade of a block or an edge of a public space. They may mandate facade materials: for example, that a certain percentage of the street facade be light-colored masonry, such as limestone. In New York City's Times Square, new buildings must have certain portions of their facades at different heights (eye level, marquee level, and distant view level), and be illuminated with kinetic (moving) signage to preserve and enhance the historic lively, entertainment character of the public space.

Clearly, zoning has a great deal to say about and exerts control over the buildings we design. This summary touches only the most basic issues. Architects who really want to influence how places look and work should participate in writing zoning law, which has a greater impact on the built environment than any individual building. From the practicing architect's point of view, particularly in cities, maximizing the potential of a client's property and simultaneously enhancing the area (which always accrues to the client's benefit as well as the community's) calls for knowledge of the complex issues of zoning to arrive at a creative solution.

Though it is not an analytic skill usually taught in architecture school, the ability to perform a thorough zoning analysis gives architects a broader range of expertise to offer clients. For example, a property owner can retain you to study potential uses of a property to determine the permitted uses and **maximum buildout** (the most floor area and best envelope configuration allowed by the zoning code) so the owner can chose development strategies for the property or understand the property's potential if selling it to someone else. You would start with the zoning map, find the district in which the site is located, and then learn the various issues as set out in the text. If the owner of an existing building wants to know how much floor area could be added under the applicable current zoning law, you can find the answer by learning the district from the zoning map and, from the text, the permitted bulk for that district. Alternatively, an owner who needs a specific use and size of building can retain you to advise what zoning districts permit that use and what size lot is needed to accommodate the owner's program requirements. In this case the starting point is the text, which specifies in which districts the use is permitted; the maps then show where those districts are located.

Architects who can supply such services are in demand in the early, formative stages of projects, which often wins them the whole project. Moreover, owners often prefer a qualified architect over attorneys who specialize in land-use law.

Building Codes

Zoning relates buildings to their larger context; building codes deal with issues of safety, health, and sanitation, ensuring that they are stable and structurally sound, provide adequate light and ventilation, can be safely evacuated in case of fire or other disaster, and are generally suitable for use and occupation. Major natural and manmade disasters—fire, flood, storm, terrorism, and design and construction errors—have caused sufficient property damage and loss of life to create the political impetus for major code revisions over the years, making buildings safer for owners, occupants, neighbors, and public safety personnel. Safer buildings undoubtedly cost more in the short run. And less in the long run.

As with zoning law, each jurisdiction selects (subject to its state's requirements) the building code it will use. Big cities have traditionally written their own building codes and developed them over decades. Many states have their own codes for residential, commercial, and institutional buildings, or combinations of these, which can be utilized by the municipalities in those states. Many jurisdictions have often chosen to utilize one of three major "model" codes: the Building Officials and Code Administrators International (BOCA), the International Conference of Building Officials (ICBO), or the Southern Building Code Congress International (SBCCI). In 2000, the three model-code writers joined to write a common model code, the International Building Code (IBC), which can be adopted as a local code as is or with location-specific modifications. Clearly, having one code for many jurisdictions makes life considerably easier for everyone—for architects, engineers, and builders who build in multiple locations and for manufacturers whose building products previously had to be designed, made, and tested to conform to the requirements of many different codes.

Many jurisdictions use multiple codes, depending on the building type and the building component or subsystem. For example, the IBC comes in different versions: one for one- and two-family houses (the International Housing Code), one for all other buildings, and one for work on existing buildings. Other codes (either parts of the IBC, or written by other national groups, such as the National Fire Protection Association, or by local government authorities) cover electrical, plumbing, energy conservation, fire, private sewage disposal, and more.

The IBC is intended to be more performance-based and less prescriptive. (If you don't remember what this means, review chapter 5, on the technical sections of the project manual.) It is intended to encourage the development and use of new design ideas, materials, and fabrication methods, making for better, safer buildings at lower cost.

Again as with zoning law, most building codes start by explaining how the code is to be administered and defining the technical terms used. Most enumerate the different **construction classifications** of buildings, from the most fireproof (no components are combustible, all structural members are well protected from fire, and some sections of the buildings are well protected from fire spread from other sections) to the least fireproof (for example, "stick-built" houses, in which all the materials are combustible and no structural or other component is safely protected from fire). Codes also typically define different types of **occupancy**, from buildings designed to be occupied by many people together in one space (**assembly**) to those for residential use or no occupants (**storage**), ordered from those requiring the greatest provisions for safety to those requiring the least.

The two sets of classifications, of construction and of occupancy, are correlated in tables showing the limitations of height (in feet and stories) and of building area per floor for each combination of construction and of occupancy. Obviously, a more fireproof building is needed for a more hazardous use, a less fireproof one for a less hazardous use, with degrees in between. Building codes often contain two such limitation tables—one for buildings that are not sprinklered,

another for sprinklered buildings. (Because sprinkler systems provide so much extra safety for a building by helping to automatically extinguish fires, the height and area limitations are considerably less stringent for sprinklered buildings than for the same combination of construction and occupancy in an unsprinklered building. These reduced limitations may more than compensate for the cost of installing a sprinkler system.) Codes also define the requirements for the design and construction of automatic sprinkler systems ("fire suppression systems") and other life-safety systems.

In some jurisdictions, parts of the territory covered by the code have access to faster and better fire-fighting than other areas, forming different **fire districts** with differing code requirements.

An important topic in building codes is the evacuation of occupants in case of fire, known as **means of egress**. Requirements vary for the construction classification, occupancy, and number of people to evacuate. Egress requirements include the number of ways out, the width and design of egress corridors and of stairways, and where the egress leads (a protected area such as a roof or outside the building). The maximum **dead-end** length permitted before offering a second choice of exit may be specified. Signage to the exits and lighting for wayfinding in the egress path are defined. And codes prescribe how much, always in terms of time (one hour, two hours), various parts of the egress path must be protected from an adjacent fire.

Most building codes specify the extent to which building and finishing materials may burn, considering how fast they will spread a fire and whether they produce poisonous gases when they burn.

The general requirements, uses, and testing of materials and equipment are also covered in building codes. Some jurisdictions require testing to their own standards; others accept testing and ratings by national organizations, either governmental or private.

Building codes define structural requirements for loading capacity, for foundations, and for all structural members and systems. They enumerate design and testing requirements against gravity, wind, flood, snow, rain, and seismic forces. Special forms of construction, such as prefabrication; special systems, such as elevators; and various building components, such as skylights, are often controlled by code, as are the requirements of ADA compliance and energy efficiency.

If building codes appear to be a major impediment to the realization of an unusual or daring design, remember: their purpose is to help you make your buildings safe. Although code writers sometimes seem like overprotective parents, their intentions and goals are similarly sound. The job of a responsible architect who wants to build something not anticipated by the code authors is to maintain the intended level of safety. Surprisingly, this can take ingenuity and invention.

Other Public Constraints

If you thought that zoning and building codes were all you have to deal with, here is some bad news: they're not. Suburban areas pose major *subdivision requirements*, including reviews and permitting processes, to achieve the communities' goals for access (both regular and emergency; some say the suburbs were designed strictly for fire-trucks), density, layout, sewage, rain run-off, utilities, and water supply.

Older towns and cities that appreciate the value of their architectural heritage to the character of their communities have enacted various kinds of *historic preservation* laws (both for individual buildings and for districts that have consistent design fabrics) and may offer incentives for preservation in tax credits or zoning bonuses. The laws may be either advisory or mandatory, prohibiting demolition or inappropriate changes except in cases of proven economic hardship. The U.S. Supreme Court has ruled that mandatory preservation acts are not a "taking" of property that requires compensation, but some local governmental entities such as city planning commissions understand that preserving old buildings can create difficulties for the owners, and these problems should be dealt with creatively—such as, for example, providing ADA access in a historic structure.

Some local governments have set up *design review boards* for new buildings and changes to existing buildings in areas that have a consistent general design style, such as all houses having clapboard sliding, pitched roofs, and six-over-one windows, even if not strictly under control of a landmarks authority. Such boards can ensure that the design is sympathetic to the context. They are often made up of local officials and architects, who evaluate each project for its look and feel rather than simply applying prescriptive rules (such as requiring pitched roofs and materials and colors that match other buildings in the area), though they do that too.

Before there were zoning and building codes and historic preservation laws, there were *private covenants* that sellers (or grantors) of parcels of land required of the purchasers. While these private covenants mostly have been superseded by governmental controls, many still exist. For example, our firm once designed a house for an owner who purchased the building lot from a seller who owned several adjacent lots and cared a lot about what he would be looking at when our client built his house. The sale included a deed restriction that required the seller's approval on the house design before construction. But what the seller had in mind was different from what our client wanted. First we designed a house the owner loved but the covenant-holder didn't care for; we redesigned it several times until we arrived at a solution both liked. Sometimes an architect can feel more like a U.N. negotiator than an architect.

Variances

Sometimes an owner's or the community's best interests or desires conflict with the zoning or building codes: an unusual use or material is contemplated; a site is so irregular in shape or topography that the normal height and setback requirements don't make sense. When compliance with the applicable laws (building *as-of-right*) can't or doesn't work, the owner can apply to the local jurisdiction for a specific waiver of that part of the law, called a *variance*. Applications for a variance may be easy (an appearance and presentation to a local planning and zoning board) or considerably more involved, requiring preparation of many forms, presentations, and appearances before hearing groups. All zoning and building codes anticipate the occasional need for exceptions and provide mechanisms for considering them.

Zoning and building codes are an engaging calculus of parts. Not all architects share this view, but accommodating zoning and building codes really can be a challenging and stimulating exercise, like a difficult puzzle.

The Future of the Profession

To paraphrase Yogi Berra: the future is hard to predict because it hasn't happened yet. Nevertheless, by looking at possible outcomes of current trends, learning from our past mistakes, seeing where others have succeeded, and learning from those lessons, as well as by speculating on what we might do better in the future, we can act to create a better future for the profession. Architects must be optimists at heart. We build for the future. We do it against great odds. We can't do either of those without a strong heart, will power, discipline, and a firm belief that the future *can* be better. However, I will begin with some pessimistic views of what the future might hold, in order to highlight some pitfalls we can take the necessary steps to avoid.

Architects may be marginalized by becoming more and more irrelevant as a result of making high design into an art form that is very expensive to build and suitable only for rare projects for wealthy and extravagant clients. Seeking to be different for the sake of novelty rather than for doing buildings better and making them more useful will diminish society's need for us and trivialize us into obscurity. The traps of celebrity and fame may distort our values and mission, and there will be fewer and fewer projects for reasonable architects to do.

Architects may become a commodity, viewed as providing the same services and distinguished only by who costs less. This in turn would lead to providing ever lower-quality services, reinforcing the idea that we are a commodity, and eventually to being indeed useless.

If architects' compensation decreases in a cost-driven profession, only those of independent means will be able to afford to practice and merit will play a lesser role, diminishing the quality and worth of what architects can give their clients.

For each of these views of doom there is an antidote. Be useful and appropriate to a wide range of clients; focus on what you do better than others, and offer those unique skills to the clients who need and would benefit from them; improve compensation by educating clients and society about the benefits that architects offer.

Here are some specific things that should be done to improve the situation and avoid the pessimistic outcomes noted above:

Teach the value that architects can add. Educate children about the built environment so they will understand the difference between bad and good design; an informed public will demand and get better design. This is true in Scandinavian countries, where design is an integral part of all children's education; the design standards there are very high for everything—buildings, products, and graphics. One can't think of this as a five- or ten-year plan, but as a long-term commitment to the future, probably a fifty-year plan.

Such programs as the New York Center for Architecture Foundation's Learning By Design program do this by sending trained architect-teachers into public schools to teach K–12 children about the built environment. AIA educational programs and general civic involvement by architects can be significant.

Improve our professional education. Change the core goal from the Howard Roark model to a more relevant, socially useful one. This is a basic change from the glorification of trends, styles, and personalities that corrosively seep through architecture school culture. Increase the attention to and time spent on technical training. In many European countries architecture students spend as much time learning materials, methods, and construction technology as they do design. We need to produce students who are substantively more expert in the technological aspects of the profession and practice of architecture. This would also help focus schools more on these issues, advancing them under more rigorous conditions than do the construction industry or the manufacturers of building components. Teach more about the related business aspects of architecture—running a practice as a business, financing and marketing projects. Students, current and future architectural educators, practitioners, and client groups should demand these changes.

Retake the leadership role of the construction industry. Provide fuller services. Architects are (or, if properly trained and motivated, would be) better trained than anyone to advise owners on *all* aspects of producing buildings, not just designing them but also getting them built well and efficiently.

Remake the construction industry. Compared to other segments of the American economy, such as manufacturing, information services, computing, telecommunications, and medicine, construction is woefully antiquated. There is very little pure or theoretical research done (other than in design theory) by the government, academia, or private industry. Compared to the changes seen in the last twenty years within those other segments of the economy mentioned above, construction has virtually stood still. It is ripe for a revolution.

I'm not talking about some more minor changes or a few better materials; I'm talking about a major top-to-bottom, whole-new-way-of-doing-things revolution, similar to the way FedEx totally rethought and changed materials delivery systems. As in that example, I believe that the construction industry revolution must come from an academic setting, combining the disciplines of architecture, engineering, business, law, economics, and politics. While the construction industry is populated by a lot of really smart people, they tend to be practical and street-smart more than theoretical. Just as FedEx grew out of a business school project and was based on a mathematical computer model rather than an examination of the existing package delivery system, the construction revolution will be based on a new theoretical model formed by the interdisciplinary groups named above, most likely in a university setting.

There are so many huge client groups that would reap substantial benefits from this revolution—government, private industry, and developers—that funding for such an endeavor should be possible if it is well presented. Whatever group makes this advance will be able to put it into action and reap the extensive rewards that will flow from revamping the outmoded construction industry. This is the real brass ring to be sought!

Forge new relationships. Instead of being the "odd group out," as we are often are, sometimes even considered a "necessary evil" or impediment to getting things done quickly and efficiently, we should always be a core, integral part of the team. While it is tempting to say we should *lead* the team, let's be a little more modest (not always our strong suit) and start off by being a better partner or part of the team. If we are useful and constructive, and if we understand (and empathize with) the goals and constraints of both our clients and their contractors, we will be well served and be able to better serve the project.

Sell ideas, not just time or services. Rethink what we are offering and how our skills should be compensated. The usefulness and joy of a building last a long time; maybe we should be rewarded for a successful life rather than just the birth. Perhaps the "royalty" model of authors of books and music, or a lifetime "use tax," are more appropriate methods than simply a one-time sale of time or services. Another model is to be a "partner" in our projects and to share in their rewards (and risks) over their lives.

Quantify the value of better design. While we know that a better-designed and better-thought-out building is easier, more efficient, and less costly both to build and to operate, without being able to really measure how much better it is hard to make a convincing argument (or sale) of the true value of better design. We know that employees in a well-designed workplace, be it a factory or an office, do better work, and that every dollar of salary paid to them produces more results; but without knowing how much more, it is a tough sale to get the client to spend more on design and on construction. Better design usually does cost a little more than mediocre design; but without being able to quantify the huge economic benefits of what we know to be a very minor additional cost, in the larger scheme and life-cycle costs of a project it is hard to convince a client to make that extra expenditure. We live in a society that believes in measuring, quantifying, and comparing results. Until we can provide those facts, it is a tough sale. With convincing facts, it should be easier to have clients *demand* better design and higher-quality buildings, rather than architects trying to talk them into it.

Make better use of CAD. While architects now produce highly accurate and data-rich drawings and three-dimensional representations of buildings in CAD, most contractors only want the paper plans that can be printed from those digital files. They end up using the same sets of paper plans they did fifty years ago! Very few constructors—general contractors, subcontractors, or fabricators—are able to directly make full use of the architects' and engineers' CAD files. Certainly, some fabricators are using digital data files for some computer-aided manufacturing (CAM), but it is still pretty rare. Someday we will send off a set of CAD files, someone will put them into a magic black box, and out will pop the building, no fuss, no muss.

Other ideas. I'm only one person; every reader of this book will have his or her own, inventive ideas. Let's combine and expand our ideas. If we focus on the goals of our profession, using all our knowledge about practice, design, technology, and building production, we will find new and better possibilities that will move us forward and return our profession to the forefront of the building industry and earn us the rewards and respect we deserve.

Index